Lyman Haynes Low

Catalogue Of The Valuable And Highly Interesting Collection

Lyman Haynes Low

Catalogue Of The Valuable And Highly Interesting Collection

ISBN/EAN: 9783741127533

Manufactured in Europe, USA, Canada, Australia, Japa

Cover: Foto ©Thomas Meinert / pixelio.de

Manufactured and distributed by brebook publishing software
(brebook.com)

Lyman Haynes Low

Catalogue Of The Valuable And Highly Interesting Collection

CATALOGUE

OF THE

VALUABLE AND HIGHLY INTERESTING COLLECTION

OF

COINS, MEDALS *AND* TOKENS,

THE PROPERTY OF

BENJAMIN BETTS,

OF BROOKLYN, N. Y.

CONSISTING OF

**EARLY AMERICAN MEDALS, STORE CARDS OF NEW YORK CITY, AND
OTHERS, EMBRACING MOST OF THE RAREST KNOWN ; BADGES
AND DECORATIONS OF THE WAR WITH MEXICO AND
WAR OF THE REBELLION, WITH MEDALETS
OF DAVIS AND BEAUREGARD,**

TOGETHER WITH A MATCHLESS LINE OF

SPANISH-AMERICAN PROCLAMATION PIECES,

FROM PHILIP V TO ISABELLA II, INCLUDING SEVERAL UNPUBLISHED, AND AN
UNRIVALLED MEXICAN ARRAY OF THE ISSUES OF MORELOS,
AUGUSTIN AND MAXIMILIAN, WITH MANY PATTERN
COINS OF THE FIRST REPUBLIC.

———▸•◂———

Which will be Sold by Public Auction at

The Rooms of the COLLECTORS' CLUB, 351 Fourth Ave., New York,

HENRY C. MERRY, Auctioneer,

TUESDAY AND WEDNESDAY, JANUARY 11 and 12, 1898,

AT TWO O'CLOCK EACH DAY,

The Coins will be on Exhibition from 9.30 A. M., to 1 P. M.

CATALOGUED BY

LYMAN H. LOW,

36 WEST 129th STREET,

AND AT

UNITED CHARITIES BUILDING, FOURTH AVENUE AND 22d STREET, ROOM 216,

NEW YORK, N. Y.

COINS AND MEDALS

(The closing number or that following name of coin)

In this Catalogue, is given in Millimeters.

(*Millimeters.*)

ABBREVIATIONS USED.

abt.	about.	*l.*	left.	sep.	separate. / separating.
Æ	Copper.	Lib.	Liberty.		
Ꭱ	Silver.	mil.	military.	std.	seated.
bet.	between.	*m. m.*	mint mark.	setd.	
bril.	brilliant.	mon.	monogram.	shld.	shield.
bzd.	bronzed.	mtd.	mounted.	sim.	similar.
Ctvs.	Centavos.	n. d.	no date.	sq.	square.
C.S.	Counterstamped.	O, / *Obv.*	Obverse.	stdg.	standing.
Cwn.	Crown.			supl.	supplement.
cwnd.	crowned.	oct. / octag.	octagonal.	sup. / suptd.	supported.
dbl.	double.				
dif.	different.	orig.	original.	Trans.	Translation.
do.	ditto.	pc.	piece.	unc.	uncirculated.
Ex.	Exergue.	pf.	proof.	v.	very.
ex.	extra.	*r.*	right.	var.	variety. / varieties.
gd.	good.	Ʀ / *Rev.*	Reverse.		
hd.	head.			W.m.	White metal.
Imp.	Imperial.	*Res.*	restrike.	wrth.	wreath.
ins.	inscription.	Rl. / Rls.	Reals.		

U. S. Mints are designated as follows: C., Charlotte; C. C., Carson City; D., Dahlonega; O., New Orleans; S., San Francisco; without letter, Philadelphia.

AUTHORITIES QUOTED.

B., Betts, C. Wyllys, American Contemporary Medals; Catalogue No. 4, S. S. & C. Co., L'd, 1892; Fis., Father A. Fischer Cat., by S. S. & C. Co., 1891; Fon., Fonrobert Catalogue; H., Herrera, Spanish Proclamation Medals; M. I., Medallic Ill. British Hist.; V. L., Van Loon, Medallic Hist. of Holland.

*** Reference in Lot 239a should be 81 not 31.

*** Lots 878 and 647 are the same piece; to be sold as 878.

*** All manner of copies, alterations and other impositions are excluded from my sales.

*** There are no duplicates in any lot unless so mentioned specially.

Copies of this Catalogue with Five Plates, giving prices realized, neatly executed in red ink, $1.00.

☞ INSTRUCTIONS TO BIDDERS.

Coins and medals are sold at so much per piece, U. S. proof sets excepted. You cannot bid for one piece in a lot. If a lot contains ten pieces, and you desire to offer $2 for it, make your bid 20c. The auctioneer will accept an advance of 1 cent up to 50c., then 5c. up to $2.50, when 10c. is the limit, up to $10, and thereafter not less than 25c. Hence any bid up to 50c. can be entertained, but after that the bid must be 55c., 60c., and so on. Such offers as 53c., $1.01, and all intermediate figures are unavailable.

INTRODUCTORY NOTE.

THE preparation of this Catalogue has been a work of peculiar pleasure and interest to me, not simply because it represents a collection of special and unusual value in itself, but also because it is a monument of the industry, judgment and knowledge of an old personal friend to whom I frankly acknowledge indebtedness for my earliest instruction in the study of Numismatics, and for advice and assistance in many of its devious and difficult by-ways. He is about to retire from the field of his activity, which he has graced for a period of nearly forty years, and now offers at public auction this splendid collection, the final witness of his long continued and critical studies in this wide domain of his favorite science.

In the following pages among his valuable, and, in a great many instances, extremely rare acquisitions, especial attention is called to the groups which, for the past fifteen years, have absorbed so large a share of his attention ; I refer to the Spanish-American Proclamation Pieces, a division in which he must be ranked as a pre-eminently distinguished authority. This lot contains an unusual number of extremely rare examples, some of which are for the first time described.

The same may be affirmed of the Store Cards, amongst which some will be noticed whose duplicates it would be difficult if not altogether impossible to find. I believe collectors will discover much that is curious, interesting and valuable, in the present collection, aside from those pieces which, from their exceeding rarity, must necessarily prove desirable for any cabinet.

L. H. L.

DECEMBER 1, 1897.

CATALOGUE.

SILVER STORE CARDS OF NEW YORK CITY.

1 Bradstreet, Hoffman & Co., etc., 1862. ℞ J. M. Bradstreet & Sons, etc. V. fine, bril. 34.   1

2 Carrington & Co., Havana Express. Mtd courier passing mile post. Unc., brilliant. $31\frac{1}{2}$.   1

3 Curtis, John K., 1859. ℞ Antiquary setd. Unc., bril. 31.   1

4 1860 Another with 9-line inscription within wrth. ℞ Bust of John Allan, a noted antiquary. Unc., bril. 31.   1

5 1861 Sim., stars over last date. "Save my Country Heaven." ℞ Bust of Washington. Unc., bril.   1

6 Ebling's | Columbian | Garden | 200 | Bowery | N. Y. Incuse stamp on S̈. 2 Rls, 1784. Good.   1

7 Another on 2 Rls. Go. mint, 1849. Good.   1

8 Finck's — Hotel. In field on a raised tablet, 21. Broad milled border, 23. Another figured 24. Size $20\frac{1}{2}$. Both unc.   2

9 Hill, E., 1860, Dealer in Coins, Medals, etc., No. 6 Bleecker St. With *revs.* Key, Phila., Woodgate, N. Y. Virtue Liberty & Independence. All incorrectly matched, as are also those in the following lot. Unc., bril. 28.   3

10 Others. *Rev.* "No pleasure can exceed" etc. Bust of jolly smoker and winged figure on dolphin. Unc., bril.   2

11 HOOKS, B.—CORNER OF ALLEN ST. In field, 276 | BROOME | STREET ℞ Bust of Franklin *l.* by *Bale.* Very fine, extremely rare. $17\frac{1}{2}$. Plate.   1

12 Horter, Chas. D., Die Sinker, etc., 178 William st. Front of building erected 1680. Unc. $25\frac{1}{2}$.   1

13 Lovett, Geo. H., Medal Die Sinker, 131 Fulton St. ℞ Brother
    Jonathan and John Bull. Unc. 31.   1
14 Lovett, J. D., Engraver Seals, Dies, etc., 1 Courtlandt St. An-
    other with New Congress Hall for obv. Unc. 25.   2
15 Lovett, R., Seal Engraver and Medalist. ℞ Bust of Franklin.
    Unc. 27½.   1
16 Meschutt's | Metropolitan | Coffee Room | 433–B⁰ Way In-
    cuse stamp on 2 Rls м̃. 1777. Good.   1
17 Metairie Jockey Club. — Member's Medal. Horse stdg r. ℞
    Not | transferable | 1851 V. fine, bril. 28.   1
    I believe this piece belongs to New Orleans. It is placed here on account of metal.

18 Model Artists.   Admit | to the | Model Artist's | 127 Grand
    St. | Near B.way Incuse stamp on 2 Rls, Zacatecas, 1820.
    Good.   1
    Prior to 1857 Spanish-American 1 and 2 Real pieces were more plentiful in circulation
    here than our own small silver.

19 Parisian | Varieties—. 16 St. & B'way. N. Y. Incuse stamp
    on Half Dol., 1875. Good.   1
20 Squire & Sons, Lewis L., Ship Chandlers, etc., 283 Front St.
    Unc. 28.   1
21 WASHINGTON | MARKET | CHOWDER | CLUB | 1818 ℞ MEMBERS
    — BADGE. Bust of Washington r. Fine, extremely rare. 23.
    Levick sale, $17.00 ; the same pc brought $23.25 in Wood-
    ward sale, Oct., 1884; Wood, 1894, $50.00. Plate.   1
22 Woodgate & Co., 1860, Importers of Brandies, etc., 83 Water
    St. ℞ Represᵗᵈ by — J. N. T. Levick. Unc., bril. 28.   1
23 Obv. as last ; revs., bust of jolly smoker. Key's Phila. card,
    and Virtue | Liberty | & | Independence; all mules. Unc. 28.   3
24 Wood's Minstrels, 1857, 561 and 563 B'dway. Admittance
    Token for 25c. Temple of Minstrelsy. Fine. 24.   1

OTHER NEW YORK CITY STORE CARDS.

Æ signifies copper, and also where the metal is not indicated, copper is to be
understood ; B, brass ; W, white metal or lead.

The dates enclosed, following the name, are established by the New York City
Directories, which give the period of the particular location named on the card, or
years of engravers when signed.

25 Admit, ℞ 1817 (2 var.) ; another, Paid, ℞ 1817. Fine. 19½.   3
    Unquestionably Park Theatre, New York, about 1820-24, notwithstanding other places
of amusement in England as well as the U. S. have been credited with it.

26 Alexander, Magician. Testimonial, 1847. Bust by *Wright.* Abt perfect, gilded. 29.   1

27 Anderson, Hy., 1837, Boots and Shoes, Chatham Sq. Unc., mostly bright. 28.   1

28 Atwood (1835–44). CARRY ME TO | ATWOOD'S | RAIL ROAD HOTEL | 243 BOWERY | AND MY FACE | IS GOOD FOR | 3 CENTS ℞ GEORGE WASHINGTON — *Bale & Smith* | *N-Y* Washington on horseback *r.* Broad, deep milling around border. Very good, uncommonly rare. 27. Plate.   1

Henry C. Atwood (familiarly known as Harry Atwood) was a gauger in the New York Custom House in 1845-46, and was also Master of the St. John Lodge of Masons.

29 Another from same dies as last, on planchet size 24, yet milled edge like the preceding. Abt good.   1

30 Another on planchet too small, though perfectly centered on gilded (before striking) planchet. Unc. 20.   1

31 BAILLY WARD | & Cᴼ· | IMPORTERS. Nᴼ· 41 MAIDEN LANE — (NEW YORK) ℞ French | and English fancy articles etc. Fine, exceptionally rare. W. 26.   1

32 BALE & SMITH | ENGRAVERS | & DIE | CUTTERS | 68 NASSAU ST (1835–38) etc. in 11 lines. ℞ From same die as 28. Unc., partly bright. Extremely rare. 26.   1

33 BANCROFT, REDFIELD. & RICE. In field, NEW-YORK ℞ Plain. Fine. Not in Holland, Levick or Tilton Collection. W. 23.   1

34 BARKER, JOHN | 16 | MAIDEN LANE | DEALER IN | MUSIC PRINTS etc., in 7 lines. ℞ American Repository of Fine Arts. Bust of Washington *r.* within wrth. Fine, but holed above head. B. 19. Plate.   1

A specimen in Levick (no other then known to Cataloguer) brought $8.25. This piece was undoubtedly the work of Wright & Bale (1829-34), and closely imitating their own and the card of Henderson & Lossing, though I judge it to be earlier than either.

35 Benziger Bros. Books Vestments Medals etc. Fine. W. gilt. S. H. Black Electrotyper. 1858 390½ Bway 1859 410 Bway 48 Lispenard 1860 142 Elm and 1861. Possibly complete original electrotypes. Mostly fine. 26, 27.   8

36 Bollenhagen, Theo. & Co. Liberty head. ℞ City Hall. Plain and milled edges. Fine, bril.. B. 19 to 34.   6

37 BONDY BROTHERS & CO. — BELT MANUFᴿˢ· NEW YORK Eagle with arrows and olive branch. ℞ Plain. Gd, very rare. B. 29.   1

It is doubtful to my mind if this piece was designed for all the purposes that others of this series were. Nevertheless it is a true card, and may ultimately have fallen to every use its present companions served. I find it in the Levick only.

38 Another. A light impression from same die as last, on obv. of
1851 Cent. Fair.   1

39 Bowen & McNamee, Silk Goods, 16 William St. (1838–43)
Cor–Beaver B. Another from different dies, " Silk " Goods in
field, Cor. Beaver omitted. Æ and B. Good to fine.   3

    Theodore McNamee, Henry C. Bowen, Saml. P. Holmes and Henry L. Stone formed
a copartnership in 1838, under the style of Bowen & McNamee, and began business at
16 William Street. In 1843 they built on the premises at 112 and 114 Broadway. Here
Anthony Gilkinson was admitted to the firm. In 1855 they built on the corner of Pearl
and Broadway. Mr. McNamee withdrew from the firm in 1858, and, after a time, he
accepted a confidential position with A. T. Stewart, and later with H. B. Claflin & Co.,
where he remained until his death in 1871, at the age of 58.

40 Bradstreet, J. M. and Son 1862 ℞ Bradstreet Hoffman and
Co. Same as 1. Æ, B. Proofs. 34.   2

41 Brewster, J. & L. — Hat Manufacturers. In field, 166 Water
St. | New York. | & | 57 Chartres . St. | New–Orleans. By
Wright & Bale (1829–34). But little circulated, partly
bright. Rare. 27.   1

42 Another, sim. to last, differently arranged, by *Bale.* V. good.
B. 27.   1

43 Buchan, David . C. | Corner of | Northmore & | Greenwich St.
℞ A chair. V. fine. B., silvered. 27½.   1

44 Another from dies of preceding, with *rev.* having ORE & over
RE & To read NORTHMOORE & Metal, size and condition as
last.   1

45 Byrne, Eleanor Rugg. Bust. ℞ Byrneore | Gold | 1859. Æ,
B. Unc.   2

46 Carrington & Co. 78 Broadway. Estab. 1857. Same as 2. Æ,
B., W. Unc. 31½.   3

47 Chisebrough Stearns & Co., Silk Goods, 37 Nassau St. N-York.
Good. B. Another sim. die, with Chesebrough and New
York. Still differing ; a new reverse, same design, Dᴿ SELLECK
in field above eagle. Æ, B. and B. silvered. 27½.   7

48 Clark, T. L. | 247 | Grand St. ℞ Manufactures — Brass Checks,
Cards &c. Fine, rare. B. 22.   1

    Thos. L. Clark, Mr. Bushnell states in his work on Cards, Tokens, etc., 1858, cut the
dies of the R. T. Thomas card. If this is a fact, then we may conclude he also cut Gosling's, Museum Hotel, Smithsonian House, Swift & Fargo, A. D. Thompson, and Upson.

49 COLLINS' READY MADE LINEN & FANCY STORE. 67 | *Maiden Lane*
℞ Ship at end of pier. Fine, rare. B. 26. Plate.   1

50 Crossman, H.—Manufacturer | No 92½ Chatham St. ℞ Female hd *l.* laur. V. fine, partly bright, as choice as I have seen. Another with eagle on rev., in same desirable condition. Low, 62, 63. S. 28½.　　　　　　　　　　　　　　　2

Henry Crossman was a manufacturer of umbrellas at 92½ Chatham St. from 1830 to 1841, after which he was located at various other places. In 1857, while at 63 Liberty St., the firm was changed to H. Crossman & Co. 1860 at 94 Warren St.

51 Curtis, John K., 1859, 83 Bleecker St. 1860 and 1861, same address, and at 882 Broadway. Jeweler and Numismatist. Antiquary setd. Busts of John Allan and Geo. Washington. Fine to perfect. Æ, B., W. 31.　　　　　　　　　　8

Mr. Curtis and Aug. Sage were the pioneers in the coin trade in this city. Mr. Curtis did not conduct public sales, neither was he actively in the field for many years prior to his death, which took place about 1890. For a long time he was in the employ of Sypher & Co., who made antiquities a part of their business.

52 Day, Newell & Day — 589 Broadway, Manufacturers | of Locks Bolts | & Hinges etc. By *Wright & Bale* (1834). V. fine, rare. 27.　　　　　　　　　　　　　　　1

53 Another from same dies in Feuchtwanger's metal. Fine, very rare.　　　　　　　　　　　　　　　　1

54 Dayton, J. H., Union Steam Washing Estab., 17th St., near 5th Ave. ℞ Female hd *l.* laur., 1837. L. 61. Unc., partly bright, a little water-stained.　　　　　　　1

John H. Dayton appears in the Directory for 1837 at above address; later as a ship-carpenter at several other locations, lastly appearing in 1852 at 141 Charles St.

55 Deveau's, P. B. & S., 156 Chatham Sq. ℞ Boot, etc., 1837. L. 74. V. fine.　　　　　　　　　　　　1

Peter B. & S. Deveau were at 156 Chatham St. 1831-50, thereafter until 1858 at 74 Forsyth St.

56 Dodge, J. Smith, Dentist. Holed, B. 24. Druidical Exhibition. B. 27. F. & M. Life Ins. Co. 1869. Æ, B., W. Fine to perfect.　　　　　　　　　　　　　5

57 Doremus, Suydam & Nixon. Dry Goods | Warehouse | N͟o. 50 & 52 | William Stͭ·. | New-York. By *Bale* (1834-40). Good, rare. 26½.　　　　　　　　　　　　1

58 Another, 209 Pearl Stͭ·. (1831-33) N-York : and Linen | Sheetings | & | Damasks in field. By *Wright & Bale.* V. good. 26½.　　　　　　　　　　　　　　　1

59 Another from same die as last, in brass. Nearly fine. 26½.　　1

60 Another, same address, with Patent | Stock | Manufactory in field. Dies unsigned. V. fine, rare. 26½.   I

61 Another as last. Æ, silvered. V. fine.   I

62 Another by *Bale & Smith*, with SUYDAMS and 37 & 39 NASSAU Sᵀ· (1835–45). Broad milled borders. Nearly fine, rare. B. 27.   I

63 Another from same dies on planchet, s. 26½. Edge milled. Fine.   I

64 Another, SUYDAM resumed. 39 NASSAU and DRY GOODS | NEW . YORK in field. Dies unsigned. Fine, rare. B. 27.   I

65 Others. Doremus | & | Nixon | 39 | Nassau Sᵗ etc. ℞ Dry Goods for | Hotels | Steamboats | & | Ships Æ and B. V. good. 27.   2

66 Others. Doremus & Nixon — 21 Park Place. Ship *r*. ℞ Stmr *r*. Æ and B. Unc. 27. Also, 1 same as 60, in brass, *rev*. worn, and another like 62 on planchet s. 24. Edge milled ; holed, otherwise v. good.   4

67 Female preventative | or | Morsonic | Amulet. ℞ Female hd *l*. wearing coronet. V. fine, rare. W. 35.   I

68 Another as last. Planchet in parts of lead and brass, the latter forming obv. and rev. Nearly fine. 34.   I

69 Feuchtwanger, Dr. L. AMERICAN | SILVER | COMPOSITION | 377 | BROAD-WAY. ℞ House & household, furniture . etc. Very fine and rare. 27.   I

70 Feuchtwanger, etc., sim. to last (Dr. L. omitted), 2.| CORTLANDT Sᵀ R From same die as 69. Very fine, rarer than the preceding 27.   I

71 1837 Eagle *l*. on rock. ℞ FEUCHTWANGER'S COMPOSITION. Oak wrth open at top, 3 | THREE | CENTS. L. 77. Slight defect on edge before eagle's head, barely reaching border milling. Very fine, and the rarest of the Feuchtwangers.   I

72 1837 Another, similar, laurel wrth and THREE | CENTS. ℞ New York State arms. L. 75. Fine. 25.   I

73 1837 Varieties of Feuchtwanger's One Cent. Eagle *r*., serpent in his talons. L. 78. Good to fine.   6

74 1864 Obv. from same die as 71. ℞ Eagle on serpent, wings spread, head turned *l*. V. fine, rare. 24½.   I

Dr. Lewis Feuchtwanger's first business location appears to have been at 377 Broadway, where he remained from 1831 to 1837; thereafter, to 1857, his changes were numerous and wide roving, considering the limits of the city within the period. He is found at 12 different addresses, ranging from No. 1 Wall Street to 21 White Street, three of which are in Maiden Lane.

75 W. FIELD — 148 CHATHAM CORNER OF MULBERRY S^{T.} in field, a hat below, NEW . YORK. ℞ A beaver *r.* Fine and very rare. 29.　　　　　I

76 Fifth Ward | Museum | Hotel. ℞ 2/6. B. 33. Finch Sanderson & C? 8th Ave Lines W. 28. Finck's — Hotel. Checks for 6, 9, 12, 15, 24 and 30 Cents in raised figures. B. 21. Fine to unc.　　　　　8

The Museum Hotel was located at the corner of Franklin Street and West Broadway. " Tom Riley," its proprietor, from 1846 to 1851, was a widely known man, and is said to have maintained a fashionable and popular establishment.

77 FRANCIS — PATENT SCREW. In field, & FANCY BOAT | ESTABLISHMENT | N°. 399 | & 402 WATER S? ℞ Francis | Patent Screw | N. York. Very good ; among the rarest. B. 26½. Plate.　　　　　I

78 Friend & Black, Electrotypers, 1860. Globe Ins. Co. 1876. Gosling's, 306 B'way. D. H. Gould, 10 Fulton St. Saml. Hart & Co. (5 var.) Fine to unc. Æ, B. and W. 24 to 30½.　　　　　9

79 GIBBS, W AGRICULTURIEST (sic) — N. YORK. Bouquet sim. to those on Montreal Sou series. ℞ A FRIEND — TO THE CONSTITUTION. A steer *r.* L. 58. Fine. Very uncommon. Plate.　　　　　I

William Gibbs, father of John Gibbs, of Belleville, N. J. (who cut the dies for and struck this token, probably between 1837 and 1840), died in 1856. He lived at 5th Ave. and 71st St., where he conducted a large flower and vegetable garden so early as 1846, and it is fair to presume from about 1837, a year or two following his arrival from England. His name is not found in the New York Directories.

80 Green | & | Wetmore | Corner of | Washington | & Vesey S! | New York ℞ Dealers — In hardware, bar-iron & steel. Anvil, hammer and pincers. B. Fine. 27½.　　　　　I

81 GREEN | & WETMORE | HARDWARE & | IRON MERCHANTS | CORNER OF | WASHINGTON | & VESEY S? | NEW YORK ℞ Spade and shovel, crossed, above anvil bet. scythe and vise, and the same die used by *T. S. Brown & Co. of Montreal.* In white metal. Very fine. I believe no more than two of these are known to collectors. 28. Plate.　　　　　I

Apollo Russell Wetmore and J. C. Green began business in 1822. They moved to address given on preceding cards two years later, where for 35 years a prosperous business was continued. Mr. Green retired in 1835, when the firm name was changed to Wetmore & Co. Mr. Wetmore died in 1880, aged 88 years.

82 Grimshaw, W. D. 1867. 15 Gold St. Card stamped by compressed air hammer. Haskins & Wilkins, 4th Ave. Line (holed). Havens, Hatter. All W. Fine. 24, 27, 38.　　　　　3

83 Hallock, Dolson & Bates 41 William St. and Hallock & Bates
234 Pearl St. 30.   A. W. Hardie Corner of Garden & Wil-
liam St. "Naked | and ye | Clothed | me " 32. All B. and
fine.   3

84 Henning, A. J., Die Sinker, 87 Fulton St. Æ, B. and W.
Unc. 25. Dr. J. G. Hewett, Bone Setter, 68 Prince St.
Good. 29.   4

85 Hill, E., Dealer in Coins and Medals, etc. 6 Bleecker St., 1860,
with 8 dif. reverses, some of which could hardly have been
struck at the instigation of Mr. Hill.   Among them are Key,
Phila., Woodgate, N. Y., etc.   A set that probably could not
be duplicated. Æ 7, B. 7, W. 8. Unc. 28.   22

86 Holmes, Booth & Haydens, nickel silver, 25. Horter, Die
Sinker, 178 William St. Æ and W. 25. Houghton, Merrell
& Co., 48 Cedar St. B. 27. Good to unc. Huyler's Candy.
Fair, holed. W. 23.   5

87 B. Hooks. | 276 | Broome | Street | Corner of Allen St. ℞
Benjamin Franklin, bust *l.* By *Bale.*   Fine, very rare.
18.   1

88 Another with impression of the "Franklin" side only. CS.
with a small dog. Fine. 18.   1

89 IRVING, L. G. below anvil, arm and hammer; above, J. S. PEASE
& Cº. Sᵀ LOUIS "He who lives by the sweat of his brow
seldom lives in ruin" ℞ Card of the house in St. Louis.
Very fine, equally rare. B. 28.   1

It is highly probable that Mr. Irving was located in New York merely as a represen-
tative of the St. Louis firm.

90 Jarvis, Geo. A. — Wine and Tea Dealer, 142 Grand St. ℞
Female head *l.* laur. below, 1837. L. 68 and 69, of same
type, but distinct vars. of obv. and rev.   Unc., partly bright ;
a very choice pair.   2

Geo. A. Jarvis succeeded the firm of Peckwell & Jarvis at 150 Grand St. in 1827. He
moved to 142, same street, during the year following, where he remained until 1838 ;
from 1839 to 1858 he is recorded at 81 Front St.

91 Jennings, Wheeler & Co., Clothing, 43 Chambers St. (5) and
later at 45 and 47 same street. 3 obvs., 3 revs., edges milled.
Æ and B. Unc. 27½.   6

92 Others, 3 vars. as last, with another having bust of Kossuth on
rev., edges plain. Æ and B. Unc.   4

-93 Others of 45 and 47 Chambers St. with bust of Lincoln *r.* and
Kossuth *l.* From Levick sale, where they brought $4.95.
Unc. B.   2

94 Johnson, Prof., Soap, Starch, Polish, etc., 317 Bowery, 1852.
Lib. hd *l.* (4) and one inscribed Prof. Johnson, another with
bust of Kossuth. Fine to unc. Æ 1, B. 5. 22 to 27½.   6

95 Jones, W^m. G. (1835–39). Union Coal Office, Corner Chamber
& Washington S! 27. J. C. Knapp Mfg C? Shell, holed,
25. Ladies Restaurant etc. 280 8th Ave. R̃ 3/6. 27. Also
La Fayette Restaurant 5 10 & 20 cts. All brass and fine.   6

96 Law, H., 187 Canal St. M. Leask, 93 Prince St. (W.) Lev-
erett & Thomas, 235 Pearl St. Fine. 28 to 31.   3

97 LEHR, F., NEEDLE THREADERS 56 CHATHAM ST. R̃ A LINCOLN
CAND'T FOR PRESIDENT — 1860 Hd *r.*, edge milled. B.
Unc., rare. 18½. Plate.   1

98 Leighton, C., 10 Park Place, N. Y., and 5 Royal St., N. O.
1st Premium Shirt manufacture. Commerce setd. R̃ Eagle.
Another with die altered to "manufacturer." R̃ Bust of Lib.
Fine. B. 22½.   2

99 Others as last described, with new rev. of the eagle type. Æ,
B. (punch on rev.) and W. Unc. 22½.   3

100 Levick (J. N. T.) 904 Broadway, 1860. R̃ "No pleasure can
exceed — the smoking of the weed." Bust of a jolly smoker.
Æ, B. (spot on rev.) and W. Unc. 27.   3

101 Loder & Co., 83 Cedar St., Jobbers of Dry Goods. Æ, B.
and B. silvered. Unc. 27½.   3

102 The same firm located at 130 Broadway. Sim. design, same
metals, condition and size.   3

103 LOVETT SEAL ENGRAVER & DIE SINKER 67 | *Maiden Lane* | etc.
in 7 lines. R̃ Ship at end of pier. Fine, rare. B. 25.   1
This card is by Robert Lovett, father of John D., Robert, Jr., and George H. The
striking resemblance of the political token (Low, No. 2) and the Collins card, lot 49 —
which has the same reverse — tells in undeniable words that all were cut by the same die
sinker.

104 Lovett, R. (Jr.) | Stone | Seal Engraver | & | Medalist | etc.
R̃ Bust of Franklin *l.* Unc. Æ, B. 27½.   2

105 Lovett, J. D. | 1 Courtlandt St. | Engraver. R̃ Wedding and
visiting cards, etc. Æ, B. and W. Unc. 25.   3

106 Others. New Congress Hall, 1860, with revs. combining both
sides of last. Æ, B. (2). 25.   3

107 Lovett, Geo. H. | Medal | Die Sinker | 131 | Fulton Street | etc. ℞ Winged figure on dolphin, edges milled. Æ, B. and W. Unc. 31.   3

108 Obv. as last. ℞ Brother Jonathan and John Bull shaking hands. Æ, B. and W. Unc. 31.   3

George Hampden Lovett was born in Philadelphia in 1824; he belonged to a family of die sinkers; his father early removed to this city, and began teaching him the art of engraving at the age of 16—a business he followed until his death in 1894.—*Am. Num. and Arch. Soc. Proceedings.*

109 Lyon, E., on coronet worn by female head *l.*, 424 Broadway. Small and large letters, 5 and 6 stars; another with name above head; also 2 smaller, 1 with bust of proprietor. Good to fine. 21½ to 27½.   5

110 Macy, R. H.— Soda Water, etc. ℞ Matthews card. Malcolm & Gaul, 62 Liberty St. Æ, B. and B. silvered. Marshall & Townsend, 7th Ave. Line. B. John Matthews, 1863 and '76. Fine to unc. 27¼.   8

111 Male Morsonic Amulet for married people. ℞ Eagle with arrows and olive branch within circle of 18 stars. Fine, rare. 34.   1

112 Maycock & Co., 35 City Hall Place. ℞ Female hd and eagle. L. 64 and 65. Unc., partly bright. Rare conditions.   2

113 Meade Bros., 233 B'way, N. Y., and Exchange Pl., Albany. B. Merchants' Exchange. L. 19, 21, 22. Fine to unc., partly bright.   4

The Tontine Coffee House in Wall Street was built in 1792, erected by the merchants, and used as a public exchange until May, 1827. The Merchants' Exchange, in Wall Street, was commenced in 1825, was completed and occupied May 1st, 1827, and burned December 16th, 1835.

114 Merritt, J. G., 12 Bowery. B. Meschutts, 433 B'way (incuse letters). Metropolitan Cave, B'way and White St. Checks for 1/, 3/, 8/6, 9/6, 11/6. J. G. Moffet, 121 Prince St. 2 var. Good to unc., 2 holed. Æ, B. and W. 27½, 28.   10

115 Merritt & Langley's, Dey St. House. Checks for 6d to 4 shil. Good to fine. Metal resembles nickel. 31.   13

116 Metropolitan Ins. Co. (3). Leop. | de Meyer's | Concert (Pianist, 22 Charlton St., 1859), holed. Wm. J. Mullin. Nat_ Jockey Club, New York, holed. Æ and B. Fine to unc. 26 to 33.   6

117 Moss' | Hotel | Cor. Bowery and Bayard. ℞ Values for 6d.
to 4/. B. Fine. 25½ to 26½.   8

118 Motts, N. Y., 1789. A clock. ℞ Eagle with arrows and olive
branch. Thick and thin planchets; various stages of die,
from perfect to badly broken. Good to fine. 26 to 28.   6

The firm of William and Josiah C. Mott is recorded in the Directory for 1789 as
clocks, etc., 240 Water St. In 1802, 49 Frankfort St. and other addresses follow, and I
believe the last vestige of the firm shows at 266 Pearl St., where they remained from 1816
to 1828. Mr. Crosby, on p. 335, " Early Coins of America," refers to this subject.

The variety of planchet with the varying state of dies is evidence of striking for
many years subsequent to date of piece. I assume the dies remained perfect until
1793, when the thick planchets were introduced to conform to the Cents issued in that
year. All defects appearing, I judge, are later impressions, while the closing issues re-
turned to thin planchets, owing possibly to the increased cost of the metal, or the
indifference of the issuer on account of local prestige and facility of circulation.

Two of the above specimens are from perfect dies — one on a thin planchet, the other
thick. The remainder show three stages of the break.

119 Mott, Wᵐ H | Corner of | Old Ship & | Water Sᵗ ℞ Anvil.
B. Others in B. and B. silvered, with L over H, correcting
SHIP to SLIP (1831). Fine to unc. 28.   3

120 N-York | & Harlem | Rail Road | Company ℞ The first type
of a rail road carriage. By B(ale) & S(mith) N-Y (1845-46).
Octagonal. Good and fine. Æ and Feuchtwanger metal.
Rare. 16.   .   2

121 Parmele. BOWLING | SALOON | KEPT BY | EDWIN PARMELE |
340 PEARL Sᵀ ℞ QUITE COMFORTABLE. Bust of a jolly
toper. Fine, uncommonly rare. From Levick's sale. B.
18. Plate.   1

Mr. Parmele was first known at 13 Park St. in 1833; he was at the address given on
card between the years 1834-38, and proprietor of the "Bowery Cottage," 298 Bowery,
1839-42.

122 Parmelee, Webster & Co., 155 Jane St. ℞ Bust of Grant,
1868. Æ and aluminum. Unc. 20½.   2

123 Peale's Museum, etc. Admit the bearer. ℞ Parthenon, 1825.
Æ. Unc. W. Good. 35. Phalon (Edward), 35 Bowery,
1837. Prescott's (Henry W.), 11 Wall St. (1847-50.) F.
metal. Fine. 17.   4

Edward Phalon probably began at 161 Chatham St. in 1834. From that time to 1860
his change of location occurred at least eleven times, and he made subsequent moves.
The height of his prosperity was reached when under the St. Nicholas Hotel, where he
remained until it closed. I had a pleasant interview with him in 1886, though he could
recall no important facts about his card.

124 Rahm, Louis, 178 William St. (1857–60). Æ and W. 25. Stephen Richardson, 177 B'way (1858–60). B. 23. W. H. Richardson, 229 B'way (1860). Æ, B. (4). 24. Fine to unc. 7

125 Rathbone & Fitch. JONATHAN RATHBONE & FRANCIS B. FITCH. PROPRIETORS — 1825. Eagle holds label, inscribed ; below, *D. Pomeroy*, 890 (engraved). ℞ Front view of a long, low building, above, CASTLE GARDEN, below, *Trested* (the engraver). I know of but four of these pieces. Fine ; brass, silvered ; (the three others are on planchets, distinctly copper. Oval. 26 x 51. Plate.

CASTLE GARDEN.

This is a decidedly interesting souvenir of a noted structure and prominent landmark in the City of New York, which still stands, though in a new dress, as a forceful memento of many varied scenes of military pageant and merry and famous entertainment.

In December, 1806, the city ceded to the National Government the ground under water on which stands the present Castle Garden. The building soon after erected on this site was named Castle Clinton, but is referred to in the Directories of the time as Fort Clinton, the cost of the work to the Government reaching several hundred thousand dollars. The structure was circular, 600 feet in circumference, the walls being 8 feet in thickness and 35 feet in height above the water, and the roof, sloping slightly from the centre, covering an area capable of holding upwards of 10,000 people.

In 1823 the Fort was receded to the city by the Government, and vacated as a military post on the 16th of June of that year, and in the May following was inaugurated as a place of fashionable entertainment under the name of Castle Garden, which it still retains. Since that time it has been the scene of many notable events. The first of these was of historic interest, being the reception of General La Fayette, "the friend of America." Here he landed from the ship "Cadmus," and was accorded a most enthusiastic welcome by an immense assemblage, in which the national and local celebrities were prominent; and on his return from Boston, a grand fête was given in his honor at the Castle, attended by over 6,000 people.

Here also, in 1850, the great "Swedish Nightingale," Jenny Lind, appeared under the auspices of P. T. Barnum, America's greatest showman, in a series of the most successful concerts ever given in this country.

Castle Garden is also known far and wide as the portal through which so many thousands from foreign lands have found the talisman of free and glorious citizenship (although perhaps, of late years, the door has scarcely been sufficiently guarded).

After these vicissitudes, it has now settled into the home of a piscatorial colony, and a place of amusement and instruction for the citizens and the city's numerous visitors.

126 Riker, Abraham, 131 Division St. (1840–49.) L. 70. J. L. & D. J. Riker, 1852 (150 Nassau St.), 2 var. B. 22. Risley & McCollum's Hippodrome. B. 32. Robinson's, Jones & Co., 1833. R. & W. Robinson, 1836. Fine. 28. 6

Mr. Riker's business record covers a long period,—extending from 1815, at 20 Suffolk St., to 1860, at 53 Canal St. During this interval he was at six other places.

127 Root & Co., 863 B'way (1854–56). Æ, B. and B. silvered. Unc. 27½. Geo. P. Rowell & Co. (1876?) B. 22½. Robt. B. Ruggles. 225 Canal St. By *Balc*, and same unsigned, each with plain and milled edge (1832–34). 28. Fine to unc.　8

> Mr. Ruggles, from 1825 to 1854, is found in the Directory at fourteen different addresses. Singularly, the one on his card is not among them. He was a colonel of the New York State Militia.

128 Royal | Preventative ℞ Eagle within circle of stars. Fine, rare. B. and W. bronzed.　2

129 Sage, Aug. B., Coins, etc., 24 Division St., 1859–60. Cards, Raffle, and Gallery Sets (the last incomplete). Æ, B. and W. Mostly unc. 16 to 31.　16

130 Another, and different, 1860. ℞ City Hall, Wall St. and Sir Henry Clinton's, No. 1 B'way. Unc. Æ, B. and W. 31.　6

131 SCHOONMAKER, W⋅ H⋅ | BROADWAY N. Y | N⁰ 181 | GUNS PISTOLS | RIFLES | &c ℞ Military Goods etc In 7 lines. Unc. B. lightly silvered. Very rare. 25.　1

132 Another, obv. as last. ℞ GEORGE IV KING OF GREAT BRITAIN. Head *l*. Nearly equal to last in condition, but in rarity it excels it. Plate.　1

133 A third variety, with bust of Jackson on rev. in oblong octagon; above, PRESIDENT. Good, but holed above head. The most precious of the Schoonmakers, and scarcely excelled in rarity by any card. Plate.　1

> Mr. Schoonmaker's record in the Directory is a short one. In 1830 and '31 he was at address given on card; in 1832, at 193 Pearl St., the location of Messrs. Wolfe, Spies & Clark (see lot 162), hence I conclude his business was absorbed by that firm, and with whom he continued.

134 Furnishing Goods | Sea | Island | & Washington | Shirts | etc. ℞ 57 | Liberty | Street. Fine, rare. B. 23½.　1

135 Scovill's, 101 William St. (1846–49.) Fine. B. Scovill Mnfg. Co., 57 Maiden Lane (1850–57). Unc. Æ, B. and B. silvered.　4

136 Smith's Clock Establishment, No. 7½ Bowery, 1837. 3 revs., 4 obvs. Good to fine.　4

> Andrew B. Smith advertised in the *New York Examiner*, June, 1837, as above, corner of Bowery and Division St., up-stairs, 3rd story, entrance 7½ Bowery. In November, 1838, the style of the firm was changed to A. B. Smith & Co.; in 1841 the partnership read Smith & Brothers, and they then announced that they had established a branch house at 9 No. Fifth St., Phila.

/ **137** Smith, F. B., & Hartman, 1860. 3 var., one with Flora Temple. B. (2), W. 28½. Jas. S. Smith & Co., 15 Dutch St. (1856–59). Address in 3 straight lines, B., and in 2 curved lines, Æ, B. and B. silvered. Decagon. Mostly fine. 22.   7

138 Smithsonian House, 606 Broadway. ℞ 135 (engraved). Fine. B. silvered. 25. Sweeny's, 64 Chatham St., 2 var. D. Sweeny & Son, 3 var., metal similar to nickel. Good to fine, 1 holed. 31. Swift (Chas.) & Fargo, 135 Fulton (1853–54). ℞ Various values (in relief), 6d to 13/. B. Fine. 27.   12

The Smithsonian House was located on the S. E. corner of Houston St. and Broadway. Later its name was changed to Revere House, and it is still occupied as a hotel.

139 Squire & Merritt, 175 South St. (1831–36.) Varieties; milled and beaded borders, distinct dies ; without number, and with number punched. Fine and unc. 27.   2

140 Squire, Louis L. & Sons, 283 Front St. (1857–60.) Æ, B. and W. Unc. 27½.   3

141 Stiners N. Y. & China Tea Co. H. H. Moses & Co., Prop's. ℞ Independence Hall and Liberty Bell (1876 Cent'l types). Unc. B. 38. Strasburger & Nuhn, 65 Maiden Lane (1853–60). Vars. Fine to unc. B. 22 to 33½.   7

142 SUYDAM & BOYD 187 PEARL ST (1831–33). ℞ Hy Suydam Wm Boyd Cloths Cassimeres etc. Fine, rare. 26.   1

143 Another, sim. design, 157 Pearl St. (1834–36.) ℞ From same die as last. Fine, rare. B. 26.   1

Suydam & Boyd, from 1810 to 1823, were at 21 South St.; 1824–28, 41 same street; 1829, 183 Broadway; 1830, 187 Broadway; 1831–33, 187 Pearl St.; 1834–36, 157 Pearl St.

144 Sweet, Ezra B., 200 Canal St., 1837, Kitchen Furniture, etc. ℞ A bold copy of obv. of U. S. Cent. L. 73. Very fine, scarce. 27.   1

Mr. Sweet's entire period is shown to have been from 1825 to 1852; during these limits, his change of address occurs twelve times. He was at 200 Canal St. from 1836 to 1839. Besides the business mentioned on above card, he is given as a Bellfounder, also Plumber.

145 Talbot, Allum & Lee, 1794. Large and small & on rev. ; one obv. die. 1795, similar. Edges differ. Good to fine.   3

146 Others. *Obv.*, Liberty & Commerce, 1794, from same die as *rev.* of first in preceding lot. ℞ John Howard. Bust *l.* V. fine ; also a stork, 1793, with 2 vars. of edge. Unc., partly red.   3

147 Taylor, G. & Son (1844–48). Taylors & Richards (1849–52 ?).
Both at 45 Cedar St. ℞ Importers | etc. One die. Fine.
Æ gilt and B. 28.   2

/ **148** Third Ave. R. R. (1853–60?) Horseless 'Bus, also Horseless Car, each with Harlem and Yorkville. Good to nearly
proof. Young & Ward, 6th Ave. Lines (1851–54), holed.
Good; all W. Tyson & Co. (1849–53.) Fine, holed. B.
All 27½.   6

149 Thomas, R. F., 247 Grand St. (1855–60.) A. D. Thompson,
25 Pine St. (1850–57). ℞ Values in relief for 1/6, 2/, 2/6.
Upsons, (Alfred A.) 349 B'way (1851–54). Good to fine.
All B. 27½.   5

150 Tredwell, S(aml.) L., 198 Pearl St. (1854.) A very rare card
but in wretched condition. Æ. 28. Tredwell, Kissam &
Co., New York Grand Canal opened, 1823. (245 Pearl St.)
B. Very fine. 26.   2

151 Tredwell, Kissam & Co. (1824–34). As last, with 228 PEARL
ST added to same die. Æ. V. good. Æ silvered. Fine. 26.   2

152 Trested, R., 68 William St. Engraver Die Sinker etc. ℞ " By
trade we prosper " on label held in talons of eagle. About
unc., very rare. B. 27.   1

153 Another. Trested | Die Sinker | etc | within wrth ; same ad-
dress. ℞ Trested Fecit. Shield within wrth. Good, holed.
rare. B. 23.   1

154 Another. Obv. same as rev. of last. ℞ SIX | CENTS. Good,
very rare. B. 23. Plate.   1

Richard Trested's Directory record extends from 1847, when at 35½ White St., to
1858 at 68 William St., where the three cards were probably issued. His name last appears in 1860 at 38 William St. Chas. I. Bushnell publishes the above tokens in his
list of N. Y. cards in 1858, but the cutting of the dies for the Castle Garden token (which
bears Trested's name) unquestionably antedates the earliest year here given.

155 Van Nostrand & Dwight, 146 Nassau St., Book Sellers | and |
Publishers etc. Æ and B. silvered. Unc. Fine. 27. C. H.
Webb, Congress Hall, 142 B'way. V. fine. 26½. Also
brass check, Congress | Hall, probably of earlier date. Gd,
rare. 21.   4

156 Vinten's D(avid) Needle Threaders, 178 Duane St. ℞ A.
LINCOLN. The same die as 97 ; three only said to have
been struck ; no rarer card, Lincoln or political. Levick
sale, $8. Good. B. 23. [See note, next page.]   1

The Directory marks the career of Mr. Vinten from 1849 to 1860, located in Jane, Mott, Elizabeth and Centre Streets, and at address on card, where he is recorded as a dealer in birds, though previously as a manufacturer.

157 Waters, Horace & Sons. H. Wellenkamp (punched). Uriah Welch, St. Nicholas Hotel. West's Trained Dogs. Æ, B. and W. Unc. 23 to 31.   6

158 WILLIAMS, R? UNION HALL | CORNER | OF | HENRY & OLIVER ST§ Heart on open hand, sep. B — Y ℞ Good for | refreshments | at the bar | Signed by *Bale*. Fine and extremely rare. Levick sale, $6.50. Æ. 19. Plate.   1

Information here is wanting, but I believe it is safe to credit the token to the same period as Hook's card, which was certainly cut between 1837 and 1840.

159 Wise, A. Wolfe's Schiedam Schnapps (1846–60). Woodcock (1856–60). Unc. Æ and W. 24 to 30.   4

160 Wolfe, C. & J. D., 87 Maiden Lane (1823–30 ?) ℞ Grand Canal, rev. same as second pc in lot 150. Fine and v. fine, scarce. B. and B. silvered. 26.   2

C. and John D. Wolfe probably dissolved on the founding of the firm of Wolfe, Clark & Spies about 1830.

161 Wolfe, C., Clark & Spies, Hardware and Military Store. Head of WASHINGTON *r.* in oval. ℞ Bust of JACKSON in oval. Good, extremely rare. B. 26.   1

162 Wolfe, Spies & Clark. Scarcely a noticeable difference from last excepting in transposition of names. ℞ Jackson in oval, with "Cutlery Plated Ware | Guns &c — 193 | Pearl . S! N. Y." added to old die. (1830–32). V. good, extremely rare. B. 26.   1

163 Obv. as last. ℞ Bust of Jackson in oblong octagonal, above PRESIDENT Fine and extremely rare. B., traces of having been silvered. 26. Plate.   1

164 Another with rev., George IV, King of Great Britain. Same die as Schoonmaker's, lot 132. V. good, extremely rare. B. 26.   1

165 Another, with Grand Canal rev., same as Wolfe card, 160. Attempted puncture, otherwise good ; as rare as any of the preceding. B. 26.   1

166 Woodgate & Co., 83 Water St., 1860. Revs., J. N. T. Levick, Jolly Smoker, Washington, Forrest, and Virtue Liberty & Independence. Æ, B. and W. Unc. 28.   13

167 Wright & Bale | Engravers | and Die Cutters | 68 William St (1829) etc. in 7 lines. ℞ Benjamin Franklin. Bust *l.* in fur cap ; below, *Wright & Bale.* Very fine and rare. B. 29. Plate. 1

168 Another of same firm at 68 Nassau St. (1832–34.) Ins. in 11 lines. ℞ Head of Washington within wrth. V. fine, rare. 19. 1

The firm of Wright & Bale — perhaps the most widely known engravers of New York City — is found in the Directories as follows : 1829, 68 William St. ; 1830–31, 16 Maiden Lane ; 1832–34, 68 Nassau St. Bale & Smith are recorded at 68 Nassau St. from 1835-38, and at 96 Fulton St. from 1840-47. James Bale is found as *Bale* on Bucklin's card dated 1834, and also on Hook's card (who was at 276 Broome St. between the years 1837 and '40), and on others as late as 1844, while he was associated with Smith ; yet *Bale & Smith* and *B. & S.* appear on others during these same years.

169 Various mules of some of the preceding, doubtless all very rare, and it is equally certain none were struck at the instigation of the proprietor of either side. Doremus & Nixon, Jennings, Wheeler & Co., Moss's Hotel, etc. Unc. Æ, B. and W. 23

170 Others, mostly of same firms, differently united. Unc. Æ, B. and W. 21

U. S. STORE CARDS AND TOKENS OF VARIOUS PERSONS AND PLACES.

171 Aulick, James. Within wreath, One | Soda ℞ Soda fountain. (Possibly Balto.) Fine and rare. Æ.16. 1

172 Ball, Danl. & Co., Grand Rapids. O. Bidwell | Middletown | U S | 1811 stamped on Cent, 1803, and U S. on rev. Bergen Iron Works Store, 1840 (2 var.) Fine. 21 to 29. 4

173 Baltimore. Champagne fountain ; Clinton Lunch (2 metals), generally attributed to Phila. (I chance it here with devices similar, some of which are equally uncertain). Columbia Garden, Cox, Haase's Park, J. E. (*rev.* eagle) and J. P. similar (each in 2 metals), Randall & Co., etc. Good to fine. Æ, Æ, B. and W. 16 to 25. 12

174 — Fasces bet. cornucopiae. ℞ Anchor. Æ. 21. Another, same design. ℞ A. McC. B. 19. Both rare, the latter especially. Fine. 2

175   BELL, A. (in script) YONKES (we must believe it intended for Yonkers, N. Y.), 1854. All retrograde, with crude attempts at ornamentation, stamped in relief on U. S. Cent of last type. Good, very rare. Plate.   1

176   Bolen, J. A., 1864 (2), 1865 (3), 1867 (2), 1869. All with bust, and 3 with his "Confederatio" rev. Æ, B. and W. About unc.; a rare lot. 25 to 28.   11

177   BRAGAW, E. & I. (1829-34), HAT MANUFACTURERS . NEWARK N. J. | AND | MOBILE | ALABAMA. By *W. & B. N. Y.* Good, extremely rare. B. 27. Plate.   1

178   Brighton Hotel (Coney Island), 5, 10, 25, 50c. Unc. B. W. R. Brown, Saratoga ; Catch Club, Phila. (city arms) ; Chapman (and others), Cinn. B. and Ger. silver. Good to fine. 18½ to 28.   9

179   Bohannan. (1843-52). DR. BOHANNAN'S MEDICAL OFFICE 63 PINE ST, ST LOUIS. In field, inscription in 11 lines. ℞ IMPOTENCY, | DESEASES OF THE | BONES, MERCURIAL | ETC CURED BY DR. B. In 10 lines. Good ; no other specimen known. W. 34½. Plate.   1

I purchased this piece in 1886 and sold it to Mr. Betts. I believe it came from the residue of Long's Museum, Phila., which was dispersed about that time. Copies of letters from St. Louis parties responding to my inquiries about the Doctor accompany the card ; one of them states definitely that it was struck in 1844.

180   BOUTWELL, O. & P. | N.º 7 | GRAND | DIVISION S.T | TROY N. Y. | 1835 ℞ Bakers & — Confectioners. By ✳ T(rue). Fine and very rare. 30½. Plate.   1

181   A specimen from the same dies, struck on a 2 Real piece of Potosi mint, 1774. Good, very rare. I have never learned of a duplicate.   1

Oliver Boutwell began as a baker at 314 River St. in 1831. In 1833 he moved to 7 Grand Division St. He took in as partner his brother, Phardice, in 1836. The following year he abandoned the baking business. In 1839 he established himself as a miller near the Sloop Lock, and continued alone until after the War. Subsequently the style was O. Boutwell & Son, and, later, the Boutwell Milling & Grain Co., which still exists. Oliver Boutwell's card is found among the little War Tokens.

182   Bucklin's Book Keeping Simplified, may be used by every one. 1834. In field, 8 line inscription. By *Bale N. Y.* Good.

I am not aware that this card has ever been classed with the rarities, but I think it significant that in a search for nearly three years I was unable to find one.

183 Bucklin's Interest Tables. Within wreath, 1835. ℞ Female
     head *r.* 14 stars around border. By *True.* Low, 10. Abt
     good, rare.   1
184 Obv. as last. ℞ Female head *l.*, without legend or stars.
     L. 12. Fair, rare.   1
185 Bucklin's Book Keeping. Within wrth, TROV. Bucklin's In-
     terest Tables, within circle of 14 stars, 1835 | TRUE ALB.
     Fine and rare.   1
186 Obv. same as 183. ℞ Same obv. of last. Fine. Also, Buck-
     lin's West Troy card, with female head. L. 13. Good.   2
187 CARPENTER & MOSHER RIVER ST Within wreath, DRY | GOODS
     ℞ Female head *l.*, inscribed Troy, same as West Troy card.
     L. 14. V. good, extremely rare.   1
188 Another as last, with 310 added below Dry Goods. L. 15. V.
     fair; even rarer than the preceding.   1
189 Childs, Mf'r. Advertising Coin, Chicago, 1863. Nickel. Fine.
     20. Jas Clark & Cº. Hudson, Clothing and Cloting. Chub-
     buck, Utica (3). Æ, B. and W. Uncirculated. 27½ to
     31.   6
190 Chubbuck, S. W., Telegraph, Chemical and Philosophical Ap-
     paratus, Utica. Unc. *Silver.* Rare. 31.   1
191 Cincinnati, 1865, Whiskey | Tax paid | Cin 475 | on one |
     barrel. ℞ Class B. Bonded Warehouse, within wreath.
     Unc. Red, extremely rare. 27½.   1
192 — Wᵐ Baker & Co. "UP," also Walnut Hills, Eckstein, Jr.,
     Evans', 64 W. 4th St., Squire, Eckstein & Co. N., Æ, B.
     and W. Round, oval and oct. Good to fine. 15½ to
     22½.   7
193 Crocker Bros., Taunton, Mass., Mnfrs. Sheathing ; Balt., Bra-
     zier's Boiler and Roofing Copper; Dimmick, Detroit; E R R
     Check ; Farnsworth, Phipps & Co., Boston. By *W. & B.*—
     N. Y. Fitzgibbon. ℞ N. Y. Crystal Palace, 1853. Fine
     to unc. Æ and B. 21 to 28½.   5

E. R. R. is probably an East Boston ferry check, entitling railroad passengers to cross
the ferry to the Eastern Railroad, whose first depot of the Western terminus was on the
East Boston side, reached by the ferry, which connected it with Boston.

194 Currier & Gre(ely) — Bo(ston) Eagle. ℞ Not | One | Cent
     within wrth. Bust just as good. V. fair, possibly as good
     as found. 28.   1

195 1855. Head *r.*, type of U. S. Cent. Heidsieck & Fils and H. Piper & Co., both of Rheims. All with *rev.* as last. Good.   3

196 FOLGER, NATHAN . C. DEALER IN | READY MADE | CLOTHING ETC | NEW ORLEANS . in 9 lines. ℞ Boys and | Children's Clothing | etc. 1837 in 6 lines. By B(ale) & S(mith), N. Y. Fine, rare. Levick's sale, $11.25. B. 34.   1

197 Foster, Martin & Co., Foster & Metcalf (2), Foster & Parry (2), Grand Rapids ; Benjn. F. Fotterall, Vicksburg (3) ; H. B. Fussell, Phila. Æ and B. Fine to unc. 20 to 27.   9

198 GIBBS, I (J) BELLEVILLE & NEW ·· YORK. U. S. M | STAGE ℞ GOOD FOR ONE RIDE TO | THE | BEARER. Good, very rare. Levick sale, $14.00. B. 23. Plate.   1

199 J. Gibbs Manufacturer . Belleville . of | Medals | and | Tokens | &c. | N. J. ℞ Ship. Low, 57. Good, rare. (See note lot 79.)   1

200 Gilbert, D. J. | Check | Good for | | Cts ℞ Harnett. | Billiard | Saloon | Market St. Wilmington N. C. N. and B. 1 holed, otherwise good to fine. Rare.   3

201 J. GILBERT, SADDLERY . N⁰ 301 | BROAD STREET AUGUSTA | GEO. By *W & B N. Y.* Obv. about good, rev. barely fair ; everything readable. An extremely rare card. Levick sale, $11.25. 27.   1

202 GOODYEAR, A. & SONS PHILAD᷅ᵃ MANUFACTURERS OF PATENT PITCHFORKS . DOMESTIC HARDWARE COMMISSION MERCHANTS ℞ Scovills | Gilt | Buttons etc. About unc., partly bright. One of the very rarest store cards, with a record of $23.00 in the Levick sale. 29. Plate.   1

203 Gotsch, A. E., 823 Walnut St. (?) W. P. Haskins, Troy (2 var.) Hopkins, Milwaukee. Hotchkiss, H. & P., Fair Haven. Good to fine. Æ and B. 25 to 29½.   5

204 Henderson & Lossing | Clock & Watch | Makers | etc. Pokeepsie N. Y. in 10 lines. By *W. & B—N. Y.* ℞ Head of Washington. Same die as 160. Fine, rare. 19.   1

205 HUCKEL BURROWS & JENNINGS . DEALERS | IN | GROCERIES | CHOICE WINES | &c &c | 1836 ℞ Boat Stores | etc. St. Louis in 5 lines. White-metal. About unc., brilliant. 29. Plate.   1

Of this extremely rare card, I know of but three other specimens, and they are in brass, one of which was in my sale of Oct. 15 and 16, 1896, and brought $9.25.

206 Jackson, C. W., Broad and Lombard Sts., Phila. Good. The same card, with Not | One | Cent. Same as lot 194 ; a mule that was never current. Jameson & Valentine, Boston. Judson, Syracuse. *B. & W., N. Y.* Kingsley, Utica and Rome. Æ, B. and W. Fine to unc. 24 to 28. 9

207 Jones | Exchange | Hotel | 77 Dock St | Phila stamped on 2 Rls, Chas. III. Holed, silver. Good. 28. 1

208 KENSETT. An ornament above and below. ℞ Same type as obv. Fine, rare. B. 23. 1

Issued by J. Kensett & Son, Baltimore, Md., who conducted a packing house.

209 Kirby House (prob. Milwaukee) ; Leask, Brooklyn ; Learned & Co., Boston ; Marshall, Oswego ; Meade & Bros., Albany. Æ, B. and W. Good to unc., most of last. 24 to 31. 8

210 KOHN DARON & CO. ℞ GOOD | FOR ONE | LOAD . within oak wrth. Fine, very rare. B. 27. 1

Location unknown, possibly Memphis, Tenn.

211 Memphis, Tenn. Drayage tickets of various firms. Fargason, Cordes & Co., Haller & Ellis, Hammar & Co., McDonald & Co., McKeen & Co., Megibben & Bro., Nevils & Rose, Paul & Crockett, values 10 to 50c. Fine to unc. Æ (2) and B. 19 to 28. 11

212 — J. W. Sheerer & Co., 10, 15, 20, 25 and 50c. Fine, and best work of series. B. 30½. 5

213 — Southworth & Knight, T. C. & Co., T. P. D., Jas. T. Ware, Wilson, Laird & Co., M. Wolf, W. H. A. & Co. Fine to unc. B. 25 to 27. 9

214 Long, E., also H. H., both St. Louis, and Wm. W., Phila., with Masonic emblems ; M(ich.). So. and No. I(nd.) R. R., Wood Tickets, ¼ and ½ cords. Good to unc. Æ and B. (1). 22 to 27. 6

215 Loomis, A., Cleveland. Eagle. ℞ Cask. V. good, rare. 30. 1

216 Lovett, R., Jr. Liberty head *l.*, 1860, same as used on his Confederate Cent. ℞ Metallic Business Cards, 200 So. 5th St., Phila. Unc. *Silver.* V. rare. 19. 1

217 — Other cards of Mr. Lovett's series. St. Geo. and dragon. ℞ Penn, eagle and wreath. Æ, B. and W. 15. (7). Another, Indian princess setd on eagle. W. 25. Abt uncirculated. 8

218 Marshall House, 1859. (Ellsworth was fatally shot in this house when descending the stairs, after having hauled down the Rebel flag.) Obv., same head as on 216. Mechanical Bakery (Boston), W. W. Messer (Boston), Myers & Co. (Phila.) Fine to unc. Æ, B. and W. 15 to 27.   4

219 Mintzer, E. L., No 2 . S. 5ᵗʰ Sᵗ Philᵃ stamped on French Sou ; Moore Bros., Springfield, Mass. ; Olcott Bros., Rochester ; Pennypacker & Sibley (Phila.?) ; Patterson, Buffalo ; Peck, Troy ; Percy & Co. Mostly fine and unc. Æ and B. 22 to 30.   11

220 N o R in monogram, for New Orleans, in oval depression, 6 x 8, CS on a *cast* 2 Reals Ṁ 1809. Fine and very rare.   1

221 — Another very differently executed mon. in oval, 8 x 11, on Ṁ Real, Chas. IV. Good, very rare.   1

222 Philadelphia. Arms of the city, supported. ℞ CORPORATION OF PHILADELPHIA. In field, ONE | SHILLING | TOKEN. Fine. SH in Shilling weak. Extremely rare. Bushnell, $41.00 ; Levick, $28.50. Feuchtwanger's metal. 26. Plate.   1

The history of this and the following piece I believe to be unknown to Numismatists. There is no doubt, however, in my mind, that they were put in use between the years 1835 and 1837, and I shall include them in my Second Edition of Hard Times Tokens. William Bellamy of New York, under date of June 28th, 1863, wrote to Geo. B. Mason, to whom he had sold one of these pieces, that he "found it in Washington Park or Parade Ground about the year 1835 or 1836." His recollection of the date was aided by the fact that he was on his way to visit the young lady who shortly after became his wife.

223 — Obv. as last. ℞ F· s· | 50 CENTS within wreath. Metal, size, rarity and condition as last. Levick sale, $28.50. Plate.   1

224 Plane & Co., Belvidere, Ill. ; Preissler, Louisville, Ky. (Æ, 20) ; Richardson, Phila. (7) Fine to unc. Æ and B. 24 to 27.   9

225 PUECH . BEIN | & Cᴼ· | NEW ORLEANS | 1834 ℞ Importers | of | Hardware | Guns & Pistols | Cutlery &c. Good. & Co. very weak, barely visible. Another card high up among the rarities. Levick sale, $14.50. Plate.   1

226 P. B. in script monogram within chain of 16 links. ℞ NOUVELLE . ORLEANS. Eagle, shield on breast ; both CS on ¼ of Spanish 4 Rl. pc. Fine and extremely rare.   1

I regard it as a most reasonable conclusion, that this and the preceding token were issued by the same firm, and possibly the 16 links establish the date of issue, as in 1834 there were 16 States in the Union.

227 Rahming, Edwin ★ ℞ LONG | ISLAND About unc. B. Very
rare. 15. Plate.   1

228 RICKETTS'S | CIRCUS Oak branches crossed below. ℞
Arms in crested shield within palm and olive branches
crossed. Very fine, extremely rare. *Silver*, milled edge.
28½.   1

229 — Another, precisely as last, in *copper*. V. fine, olive shade.
Plate.   1

230 — Another, like the preceding, with edge plain struck on a
much thicker planchet ; barely evidence of even handling ;
a medium brown. 28.   1

Ricketts's Circus has generally been catalogued as a Philadelphia Token, although
New York and also Boston claim its paternity. Washington was one of its patrons in
Philadelphia. It was located at 12th and Market Sts. from October, 1792 until the spring
of 1795, when it went to Boston. It is recorded that " Rickett's Amphitheatre offered t o
exhibit one evening for the benefit of the poor (of New York city) to purchase firewood,
which was accepted by the corporation, and the sum of $340 was collected on the occa-
sion." It was destroyed by fire in Philadelphia in December, 1799.

231 Robinson, Chittenango ; Rogers & Bro., Gloucester, Mass. ;
Ross, Drugs, Cinn. ; Safford, Albany ; Seeger, Balt. ; Smith,
Windsor, N. Y. ; Snyder & Shankland, Phila. Good to fine.
Æ, B. and W. 20 to 33.   8

232 Roxbury — Coaches ℞ New Line 1837 V. good, scarce. F.
metal. 18½.   1

233 RUSSELL, R. E. | I · O · U | 12½c. ℞ Eagle, etc., 1837. From
one of Feuchtwanger's dies. Fine, very rare. F. metal. 19.
Plate.   1

234 Scovill's, J. M. L. & W. H., Waterbury | Con. | etc. in 9 lines
within wrth. ℞ ESTABLISHED 1804 ENLARGED 1812 | BURNT
DOWN MARCH . 1830 . | REBUILT JULY | 1830. View of fac-
tory. Very fine, exceedingly rare. W. 45.   1

235 Seaman, T. D. Butcher — Belleville. Bouquet, closely resembling Le Roux 517 to 524. ℞ A Friend — to the Constitution. A steer *r.* Low, 59. Fine, rare.   1

236 Starbuck, N. & Son, Troy. ℞ A screw-bolt. Starr, Buffalo ;
Stephenson's, do. ; Thompson, do. Good to unc. Æ, B.
and B. silvered. 21 to 37.   8

237 — Starbuck's rev. (screw-bolt). ℞ Female head *r.*, Troy on
coronet. Good, rare. Low, 11.   1

238 Stevens. PAY | THE BEARER ON | DEMAND | ONE DOLLAR |
AND CHARGE THE SAME | TO | JOHN STEVENS | JUNE 20 1829
| TO JOHN V. BOSKERCK | FERRY MASTER | *W & B* ℞ One |
Dollar | payable in | specie . within wreath ; below, *Wright
& Bale* About unc. No rarer store card ; none more
highly prized. Levick sale, $31.00. Brass. 21. Plate.   1

239 St. Louis Post Office. Above, eagle on shld draped with
flags. ℞ *Lepere | & Richard* (engraved script). By *J. M.
Kershaw.* Holed near edge. Unc., very rare. W. 24.
Another and dif. design, eagle *l.*, by *Stubenrough & Weber.*
℞ *Hume & Co.* (script.) Good. Æ. 28.   2

239a Thomas & Co., H. E., Wholesale | Hardware Store | Main |
near Wall S�°ₜ | Louisville | K⸁ ℞ Spade and shovel crossed.
Same die as rev. of lot 81, which see. White-metal. Unc.
No rarer card exists. I do not know of a duplicate. 28.
Plate.   1

240 Tilly Haynes & Co., Springfield, Mass. B. (holed), White-
metal. Troemner, Phila. ; Willard, Boston ; Wolff, Peters-
burg ; Yates, Syracuse. Æ, B. Fine to uncirculated. 19 to
28½.   10

241 Twigg, G. S.— Hastings Hotel. In field, 3ᴰ ℞ Eagle with
arrows and olive branch in talons, 16 stars around border.
V. fine. Brass. 28.   1

This token is placed here, solely for the reason that its rev. is so distinctly and em-
phatically American. L. J. Durkee was another proprietor of this hotel and issued a
similar piece with the same rev. die.

242 Walsh's Gen! Store Lansinburg and Lansingburgh. 3 var. Gd
and fine.   3

Alexander Walsh was, for upwards of 40 years, one of the most prominent merchants
i n Rensselaer Co. His store was widely known as "Walsh's Museum"; his "Plough
Penny" circulated freely through all of Northern New York; he participated in the
ceremonies on the opening of the Erie Canal, by invitation of Gov. De Witt Clinton,
whom he accompanied on the first boat, and received with the other guests a silver
medal commemorating the occasion. He entertained Henry Clay at his home in 1839;
i n 1846 he retired from business and died three years later.

243 Waterbury House, 42 Church St., N(ew) H(aven). By *W B D*
℞ 4 with two small hounds running *l.* Fine, rare. B. 20.   1

244 Williams, Geo., Belvidere, Ill. ℞ Amsden's Genoa card, man
running *r.* Struck on Ṁ 1 Real, 177(8). Fair ; very rare.
Ꞃ. 21.   1

245 YEATMAN & CO., J & B 13 stars around border. GOOD FOR |
TWO | BITS ℞ Eagle with shld on breast, arrows in his *r.*
talon, olive branch in *l.* V. fine, partly bright, exceedingly
rare. 25. Plate.   1
Possibly Portsmouth, Norfolk, or Richmond.

MISCELLANEOUS.

246 **Indian Traders.** E. H. Durfee, 50c. ℞ Steamboat. Lee
& Reynolds, Ind. Ter., $1.00, also "Trade Check" and
"Trade Mark," each with a plunging buffalo on rev. Good
to unc. N., Æ and B. 24 to 31.   4

247 McClure, E. A., 25 and 50c. J. S. McCormick, Ft. Laramie.
℞ Liberty, 25 stars around border (holed). N., Æ and B.
23 to 33.   3

248 **Location Unknown.** Bouchman Bar, by E. L. Brockway ;
J. C. Burden, Copper Mine Token, 1c., 1860 (Indian and
Lib. hd), John Eichler, H. H. Elliott, Emmitt House, Bren-
ham, Col. Hardy, C. M. Harris, John J. Horn, Kendall's.
Mostly fine. Æ, B. and W. 17 to 28.   13

249 H. Y. Lefevre, 49½ N. Main St., 1864 ; Lynn House, Mechanics'
Savings Bank, I. Michiner, Geo. Percival & Co. (holed), F.
E. Richard, Yankee Robinson, Tieman's, J. C. Tilton (Æ,
19), Weighell & Sons, J. B. Wilson's. Good to fine. Æ, B.
and W. 16 to 27.   13

250 **Initials.** S S B | 1837 ℞ Border of leaves. Fine, rare. 19. 1

251 L. K., another Lanc | L. K., ticket for shave, by W. H. M.
Others, J. H. & Co., V. L. C., etc. Two have value only,
12 cts and 37 cts, within shld surmounted by eagle. Good
to fine. Æ, B. and W. 15 to 30.   13

252 **Omnibus.** Accommodation Line. Octag. ℞ B. F. Z. & Co.
Durkee & Co. Two asses braying, "When shall we three
meet again." F. H. F. & Co. (holed), J. Mitchell, etc. In-
cludes 1 of Stockholm. Good to fine. Ger. sil., Æ, B. (5
oval.) 18 to 26.   11

253 Watchmakers' Checks, Ice Tickets, etc. Good to fine, 7 holed.
Mostly brass, with 3 foreign cards, 1 choice. 22 to 29.   18

254 **Stamped** (incuse) Cards, Checks, Tickets, etc., among which
USE | G G G | & | G G G G on a v. good 1798 Cent, J. T.
S. | 1830 etc. Very few with address. A variety of shapes,
sizes and metals, 2 holed.   34

255 **Calendars.** 1845–46, S. H. Gilman, Boston, maker; 1852,
     Demarest, N. Y., both W., 39; 1853 and 1853–54, J. B.
     Hyde, N. Y., B., 37, 34; 1853, H. W. Sabin, B., 44. Mostly
     fine.   5

256 1853, H. S. Banks, by H. A. Clum & Co.; S. Smith, Spring-
     field, Mass., Publisher; R. Paine, *Sculptor*, both W., 45;
     1854–55, T. S. Sperry, N. Y., B., 34; also Hyde, same date,
     Æ, 34; 1855, Hyde, also Sperry, B., 34. Mostly fine.   6

257 1855, State arms, N. Y., Penn. and Ohio, *rev.* movable cen-
     tres; 1856, J. B. Person, 346 B'way, N. Y.; also perpetual
     devices by Jas. Tipping, Winchester, Va.; one has card of
     Henry Robinson & Co., N. Y. Fine to unc. B. 5, W. 1.
     35 to 45.   6

258 **Diverse.** (1736) Auctori Plebis. Bust *r.* ℞ Blank. Good,
     rare. 26.   1

259 1755 Lud. XV, etc. Bust *r.* ℞ Non vilius aureo, a galley.
     Good. 28.   1

260 1786 W. Bass (script). ℞ Wrecked ship, not unlike Hard
     Times Token design, all engraved. Good. 27.   1

261 1786 New Jersey Cent. Maris, 18.j. Extremely fine and
     sharp impression, slightest marks of circulation; a light
     brown. Very rare. Dr. Maris says in his work, "I have
     seen but three."   1

262 1787 Another, M. 63 s. Very good.   1

263 1795 Half Cent, struck on a planchet, which shows it to be a
     Talbot, Allum & Lee.   1

264 1839 United States of America. Eagle on portion of globe.
     ℞ Exploring Expedition. In field, u. s. ship | peacock |
     1839 The last 2 lines stamped; holed near edge, otherwise
     fine, rare. W. 25.   1

265 — Another as last, with subjoined stamping. Holed, fair.   1

266 1853 Two obv. and two rev. impressions of United States
     gold Dollar on obv. and rev. of м̃ 2 Rls, 1867. Fine and
     remarkable.   1

267 Duplicates of Store Cards, one so good as W. H. Schoon-
     maker. There are also 12 mules, some curious and un-
     fitting combinations, no doubt all unknown to parties whose
     names they bear, and difficult now to duplicate. Æ, B. and
     W.   21

268 Barnum's Museum. Tom Thumb and his parents; H. G. Sampson's medal card, etc. Æ, B. and W. 22 to 42, mostly above 38.   10

AMERICAN MEDALS.

Æ, Silver. Æ, Copper. W.m., White metal. B., Betts, Am. Col. History illus. by Contemporary Medals. V. L., Van Loon. M. I., Medallic Illustrations of British History.

269 1628. PET : PETRI : HEINIUS . etc. Bust of Heyn facing, in armor, wearing high ruff and quadruple chain. ℞ HEINIAD NVP SENSIT SPOLIATA MATANCA. View of the capture of the Spanish galleons in the harbor of Matanzas. B. 26. V. L. II, 171. Very fine, very rare. Æ. 60.   1

270 (1665) JACOBVS ˙ DVX ˙ EBOR ˙ ET ALBAN ˙ etc. CAROLI ˙ II ˙ REGIS. Bust of the Duke of York r. by *Roettier.* ℞ GENVS ˙ ANTIQVVM An antique trophy. Naval engagement in the distance. V. L. II, 505. M. I. I, 505. Very fine, rare. Æ. 64.   1

This medal commemorates the naval action off Lowestoft, June 3, 1665, against the Dutch. The English were successful under James Stuart, Duke of York and Albany (afterwards James II). It is placed here by reason of Albany and New York having been named in his honor in 1664, up to which time they were known as New Orange and New Amsterdam.

271 1667. BRITAN : BATAV : PAX Shields of Great Britain and Holland suspended through wreath. ℞ An English and a Dutch ship sailing amicably side by side. V. L. II, 538; M. I. I, 535. About perfect, rare. Æ. 44.   1

Refers to Peace of Breda and alliance of England and Holland, when New York was confirmed to England. Therefore this medal, having direct reference to America, was overlooked by Betts.

272 1738. V. LVSTR : FŒD : BELG : etc. Female setd before Temple of Janus, Belgian lion at her side, Fame flying above. ℞ ORBIS CHRISTIAN : etc. Shields of Britain, Germany, France, Spain, Portugal, Denmark and Poland. V. L., Sup. XIV, 127; M. I. II, 525. About perfect. Æ. 56.   1

This medal was struck upon the 25th anniversary of the Peace of Utrecht, when the enlargement of British Colonies and Plantations in America was secured.

273 1758. Louis XV. Bust r. ℞ WESEL, OSWEGO, PORT MAHON Four island forts ; below, EXPUG . Sᵀᴱ DAVIDIS | etc. in three lines. B. 415. About perfect, very rare. Æ. 31. Plate.   1

Refers to capture of Oswego, N. Y., Wesel, on the Rhine, Port Mahon, Minorca, and St. David's, on the Coromandel Coast.

274   1762. EVROPAE ALMAM etc. Indian with bow and quiver
      holds Cupid, who places figure of Peace on column. ℞
      DVRET VSQVE etc. Mercury setd on Belgian lion, before
      marine view. B. 442 ; V. L. Sup. 365. About perfect, rare.
      Æ. 44.   1

275   1777. B. FRANKLIN ' OF PHILADELPHIA L. L. D. & F. R. S.
      Young bust facing, head turned slightly *l.* wearing a loose
      cap. ℞ NON IRRITA etc. A tree struck by lightning from
      cloud *l.* B. 547. Fine, extremely rare. Æ. 45. Plate.   1

276   1777. B. FRANKLIN . AMERICAIN . Bust *l.* in fur cap. By *Nini.*
      ℞ Plain. Perfect, extremely rare. Terra-cotta, 114. (See
      note, B., page 247.)   1

277   1781. INJVRIIS COACTA Holland symbolized by female stdg,
      lance in hand, before Batavian lion on anchor, etc. ℞ IM-
      MORTALIBUS BATAVVM etc. 7 laurel wreaths on glory of rays,
      each inscribed within. Refers to the battle of Doggersbank.
      B. 589. Extremely fine. Æ. 45.   1

278   1781. LIBERTAS . AMERICANA . Hd of Liberty *l., ex.* 4 JUIL.
      1776. ℞ NON SINE etc. Minerva with shield and lance repels
      the British lion. *Ex.* $\frac{17}{19}$ OCT $\frac{1777}{1781}$ B. 615. Fine, and
      without the small breaks in *ex.* on obv. commonly found on
      specimens. Very rare. Æ. 48.   1

279   1782. Frisian stdg between two females, each hold shield ;
      the one *l.* inscribed DE | VER | EENIG | DE | STAATEN | VAN |
      NOORD | AMERI | CA ℞ AANDE STAATEN VAN FRIESLAND
      etc. in 8 lines. B. 602. Extremely fine, rare. Æ. 44.   1

280   1782. LIBERA SOROR Female *l.* in armor grasps hand of Indian
      queen *r.* over burning altar. ℞ TYRANNIS VIRTUTE etc.
      Unicorn lying against high rock *l.* B. 603. About perfect,
      brilliant, very rare. Æ. 45.   1

281   1782. FAVSTISSIMO FOEDERE etc. Fame setd on cloud, sup-
      porting two shields, one charged with 13 stars (for the
      United States). ℞ JUSTITIAM etc. Monument *l.* Mercury,
      flying, placing wreath on Amsterdam shield ; anchor and
      basket of fruit *r.* B. 604. Extremely fine, brilliant, rare.
      Æ. 45.   1

282   1782. Another of same type on smaller planchet. B. 605.
      A very slight nick in field, otherwise about perfect. Æ.
      34.   1

283 1782. EN DEXTRA etc. Holland std, receives olive branch from man carrying the U. S. flag. ℞ HEIL, VRIJGESTREEN | etc. in 8 lines. B. 606. About perfect, very rare. Æ. 32.   1

284 1782. NEDERLAND VERKLAARD AMERICA etc. Female stdg. ℞ Erect trident holds flags of Holland and the United States wing and wing. B. 607. Extremely fine, brilliant. Æ. 34.   1

285 1782. Another from same dies as last, but in bronze. Perfect. 34.   1

286 1783. LIBERTAS AMERICANA Louis XVI setd at *l.*; before him, Liberty hangs shield charged with 13 bars on column. ℞ Pallas stdg, holds 5 shields. B. 608. V. fine. W.m. 45.   1

287 1784. Female stdg on pedestal inscribed RES | PUBLICA | AMERI | CANA 4 small shields suspended from garland, *ex. B. C. V. Calker F.* ℞ Hand from cloud returns sword to its scabbard, on which a label inscribed PAX; below, RESTAURATA MDCCLXXXIII | & MDCCLXXXIV Commemorates the Treaty of Paris. B. 613. Very fine. I believe this has appeared but twice before in an American catalogue, the last time in 1890, when it brought $40.00. W.m. 40. Plate.   1

288 1792. Liberty head *l.* by *Galle*, closely resembling that of lot 278, by *Dupre*, for which reason alone it is placed here. National convention of artists at Lyons. Very fine. Bellmetal. 38.   1

289 1796. Castorland . Franco-Americana Colonia. Head *l.* with chaplet, wearing civic crown. Milled edge. Bzd proof, a few light stains. 31.   1

290 1796. Another from same dies as last. Milled edge, brass. Unc., slight blemishes. 32.   1

291 Washington. Head *l.* ℞ A star within a radiation. Fine, rare. Æ. 11.   1

292 THE ˙ THEATRE ˙ AT ˙ NEW ˙ YORK ˙ — AMERICA. Front view of old Park Theatre. ℞ MAY . COMMERCE . FLOURISH . Marine view, cornucopia and emblems of commerce on shore ; edge, I promise to pay on demand the bearer One Penny. Æ. Unc., partly bright, very rare. 35.   1

The Park Theatre, which this token is generally believed to refer to, was commenced June 1st, 1795, and completed in 1798. The proprietors petitioned for permission to erect a portico over the sidewalk, but it was not granted. The theatre was burned May 25th, 1820 (also in 1821, according to one authority). In February, 1824, a grand ball was given for the benefit of the Greeks, when $2000 was realized. A third conflagration of the theatre took place Dec. 16th, 1848.

293 PRESIDENT OF THE — AMERICAN FUR COMPANY. Naked bust
     of John Jacob Astor *l.* ℞ FORT UNION — U. M. O. A pipe
     and tomahawk crossed above and below, two right hands
     clasped, PEACE AND FRIENDSHIP. Has probably passed
     through fire, leaving surfaces lightly pitted; it is not im-
     paired, however, to rate below fine. Æ, silvered, and sub-
     sequently gilded. Of the highest rarity. 65. Plate.   1

This very rare and highly interesting American Indian Medal, unknown to the fraternity of coin collectors until about the year 1885, was probably struck between the
years 1806 and 1811. The design of the Indian medal inaugurated in the time of President Adams was probably its prototype, and as it was to serve a similar purpose among
the Indians, its strength as a seal to friendship, was probably designed by the promoters
to be of equal consideration. For a full account of the medal, see A. J. of N. for July,
1897.

294 1837. Centen! Celebr! of S? C? Society Mar. 28. Hand hold-
     ing 3 grape-leaves. ℞ Was admitted | a member | etc. in 4
     lines. About perfect. Æ. 32.   1

295 State of Louisiana to Maj. Gen. Zachary Taylor. Pelican
     feeding her young. ℞ Battle scene. Monterey — Buena
     Vista — Palo Alto, etc. V. fine, scarce. Æ. 77.   1

296 Bust of Gen. Taylor *r.* by *Wright.* ℞ "A little more grape,
     Capt. Bragg," etc. Perfect. Æ. 33.   1

297 1846. Mil. bust of Taylor *r.* ℞ Resolution of Congress,
     Palo Alto, Resaca de la Palma. V. fine. Æ. 65.   1

298 1847. Bust from same die as last. ℞ Resolution of Con-
     gress, etc., Monterey. Perfect. Æ. 65.   1

299 1847. Winfield Scott. Bust *l.* on inscribed tablet. ℞ From
     Virginia. Column surmounted by eagle. Nearly perfect.
     Æ. 90.   1

300 1848. Naked bust of Scott *l.* by *Wright.* Seven battle
     scenes, City of Mexico in centre. Perfect. Æ. 90.   1

301 1848. Maj. Gen. Taylor. Naked bust *r.* by *Wright.* Res.
     of Congress. ℞ Scene of battle of Buena Vista within
     circle formed by 2 serpents. About perfect. Æ. 90.   1

302 1849. Presented to Lieut. Col. Bliss of the U. S. A. — For
     his gallant services in Mexico | by the State of New York.
     Bust *r.* by *Wright.* ℞ State arms and names of battles.
     Nearly perfect, rare. Æ. 70.   1

302a 1850. JENNY LIND Head *l.* ℞ 12.500 Dollars given by
Miss Lind to Charitable Institutions. First Concert in
America | ✳ | at Castle Garden | N. Y. Sep. 11 . 1850 | at-
tended by | 7.000 people | proceeds . 35.000 Dollars. Very
fine and rare. W.m. 42. Plate.   1

303 1859. JOHN BROWN, etc. Bust facing slightly *r.* by *Würden.*
℞ A LA MEMOIRE | DE | JOHN BROWN | ASSASSINE JURIDIQUE-
MENT | A CHARLESTOWN etc. in 11 lines. Nearly perfect.
Very rare. Æ. 58.   1

304 1860. Bust of Washington *r.* ℞ Washington. Cabinet of
medals, U. S. Mint, etc. Perfect. Æ. 60.   1

305 1865. ABRAHAM LINCOLN etc. Bust *r.* by *Bovey.* Born Feb.
12th 1809 Died assassinated April 15th 1865. ℞ Emancipa-
tion | of Slavery etc. in 4 lines. Encircled by gilt convex
band, designed in oak-leaves depending from eagle, with
ring. Perfect, rare. Æ, 70.   1

306 1865. SALVATOR PATRIAE Bust of Lincoln *r.* by *Sigel.* ℞
IN MEMORY | OF THE | LIFE ACTS AND DEATH | OF | ABRAHAM
LINCOLN | etc. in 8 lines, within olive wreath. Published by
the Am. Num. and Arch. Soc., 1866. Nearly perfect ; very
thick planchet. Rare. Æ. 84.   1

307 1865. Another as last, but in white metal. A few slight edge
dents, otherwise about perfect. 83.   1

308 1865. Others of same design, issued under the same auspices ; size reduced to 36 mlm. Æ, Æ and W.m. Perfect.   3

309 1865. Others, reduced to 16 mlm. Metals and condition as
last.   3

310 1866. MAJ: GEN⋮ GEORGE G. MEADE. Head *r.* Presented July
4th by the Union League of Phil⋮ | as a token of the grati-
tude of his countrymen. ℞ Columbia setd presents wreath
to Gen. Meade. The Victor at Gettysburg, etc. Perfect,
rare. Æ. 80.   1

311 1867. CYRUS W. FIELD. Head *l.* on cloud above ocean, ship
l., steamer *r.* Honor and fame are the reward. ℞ By resolution of the Congress of the United States, March 2,
1867, for his foresight, faith, and persistency in establishing
telegraphic communication, etc., in 13 lines. Perfect, rare.
Aluminum. 103.   1

312   (1868.)   Edward — Willis Parsons — of Flushing, New York.
Crested shield with arms. ℞ Eliza — Ferris Anna — Ferris |
Oct. 1768 (the 7 and 6 are joined) 5ᵗ\ʰ | Mary — Ferris
Taber | of Throgg's Neck | N.Y. | Memento from | I. F. W.
Æ. Proof, rare. 27½.   1

313   (1868.)   GENERAL U. S. GRANT Bust facing, head slightly *r.*
By *Bovey.* ℞ I intend to fight it out on this line if it takes all
summer. In field, Patient of toil | serene amidst alarms. |
etc., in 4 lines. Encircled with band, same as 305. Perfect,
and *much* rarer than the one with bust *l.*, having same rev.
Æ. 70.   1

314   1876. United States of America. Heraldic eagle. ℞ To
Peace and Commerce. Mercury stdg before Indian princess
setd. *Ex.* IV JUL. MDCCLXXVI. Copy of *Dupre's* medal by
C Barber — 1876 Perfect, rare. Æ. 67.   1

315   1876. Memorial Hall — To commemorate the Centennial |
Anniversary of the | United States | Phila July 4 | 1876 ℞
Independence Hall. About perfect, brilliant. Æ. 58.   1

316   1876. Art Gallery. *Ex.* Fairmount Park | Philadelphia. ℞
The Main Building. Perfect. Æ gilt, proof. 51.   1

317   1881. President of U. S. A. Head *l.* ℞ In | memory of |
J. A. Garfield | Sept. 19. 1881. Perfect. Gold. Die pro-
jecting loop. 12.   1

318   1881. Eagle on shield beside obelisk, on radiated field. ℞
Presented to the U. S. by Ismail, Khedive of Egypt, etc.
Perfect. In orig. paste-board case. Mr. Hewitt's presen-
tation on behalf of the Am. Num. and Arch. So. Very rare.
W.m. 41.   1

319   1883. CHARLES EDWARD ANTHON. Head *l.* by *Ahlborn.* ℞
Pres. Am. Num. and Arch. Soc'y, 1869–1883. Oak and
olive wreath and society seal. Born in | New York City |
Dec. 6. 1822. | Died at Bremen | June 7. 1883. A beautiful
medal. Perfect brilliant proof in silver. Less than 12 struck
in this metal. 68.   1

320   1883. Another, from same dies as last. A bronzed proof ; 67
struck. Perfect. 68.   1

321   1883–89. Brooklyn Bridge, Bartholdi Statue, Firemen's Souvenir, etc. Perfect, 4 holed as issued. Brass and W.m.
22 to 38.   5

322 1886. Bartholdi. Head *r*. ℞ Statue of Lib. enlightening
    the world. Perfect. Æ and W.m. 38.   2

323 1886. Albany. 200th Anniversary. City arms. ℞ Scene
    of receipt of charter. Perfect. Æ. 51.   1

324 1889. Pittsburgh | "Gas City" — Chamber | of Commerce.
    ℞ National American Conference. Bar inscribed SOUVENIR
    Perfect. Æ gilt. 45.   1

325 1889. GEORGE . WASHINGTON . Bust *l*. by *St. Gaudens*. ℞
    To commemorate | the inauguration | of George Washing-
    ton | as first President etc. in 12 lines. Perfect original
    bronze cast. 115.   1

326 Franklin, Washington, Jefferson, etc., to Lincoln. Perfect.
    W.m. Oval and circular. 23. Only about twelve sets
    struck.   12

327 Decatur, McDonough, Munro (sic) and Perry in field, branch
    above and below. ℞ Eagle. Fine, rare. Brass. 17½.   4

328 **Coins.** Small Cents. 1857, '58, '59 (proof), '62, '63 (proof),
    '64, '82, '86. Unc.   9

329 Two Cents. 1864, '65, '66, '67, '68, '69, '71. Unc., mostly
    bright.   7

330 Three Cents, silver. 1851, '52, '53, '54, '55, '58, '59, '60, '61,
    62. Good to unc.   10

331 Nickel. Three Cents. 1865, '70, '73. Five Cents. 1866,
    67, '68, '69, '72, '82, '83. Uncirculated.   12

332 1892. Proof set, 1, 5, 10, 25, 50 Cts. and Dollar.   1

ORDERS, BADGES, ETC., AND MEDALS BESTOWED UPON SOLDIERS AND SAILORS.

333 Pitt Club. NON · SIBI SED · PATRIÆ · VIXIT White cameo bust
    r. on black. ℞ In memory of the R! Honble Wm Pitt Died
    23 Jany 1806 aged 47 Inscribed to *Sr Robt Vaughan Bar^t
    M. P.* Oval, 29 x 35, attached to branches crossed. Loop,
    ring and ribbon. Point of bust broken off, otherwise fine,
    rare. Æ gilt.   1

334 **War with Mexico.** 1846. VETERANS OF THE MEXICAN |
    WAR. Fortress on hill *r*., below a piece of artillery, at *l*., a
    man-of-war. ℞ Plain, with hinged pin and catch, shield
    shape, 32 x 35. Very fine, very rare. Æ. Plate.   1

335 1846 MEXICO above nopal plant at opening of wreath ; below, fortress and date ; above, muskets and sword crossed bet. cannon *r.*, and man-of-war *l.* Around border, TOBASCO — VERACRUZ — PALO ALTO etc. ℞ Engraved in script, John S. Lynch | Co. K. 11ᵗʰ Inf. Shield shape, 31 x 35. Loop and ring. V. fine, rare. Æ.   1

336 1846 Another, same design. ℞ Plain, with bar near top for ribbon. V. fine, rare. Æ. 41 x 45.   1

337 1846. Another, same design. ℞ Engraved script, John S. Lynch | 11ᵗʰ Inf Perfect, rare. Æ. 54 x 58.   1

338 Presented by the City of New York — To the N. Y. Regiment of Volunteers in Mexico. State arms. Engraved in field in script, *John Boyce Company K.* ℞ Chapultepec, Cherubusco, etc. America hurls thunderbolts at Mexican forts. Fine, swivel ring attached to edge. Æ. 52.   1

339 Another, from same dies as last, in bronze. Abt perfect. 52.   1

340 1846–47. South Carolina to the Palmetto Regiment. Palmetto tree, trunk bet. shields. Engraved in script, *Corpʔ James F. Quinn.* ℞ Vera Cruz, Contreras, etc. Land and sea assault on forts. Perfect. Æ. 48.   1

341 Presented by the Citizens of Charleston — To the Charleston Company of the Volunteers in Mexico. Columbia setd in Charleston harbor. By *Wright.* ℞ Vera Cruz ★ Cherubusco ★ Chapultepec ★ Garita de Belen. Officer with flag stands in captured fort. Perfect, extremely rare. W.m. 55.   1

342 **War of the Rebellion.** ARMY OF THE | CUMBERLAND in depressed oval within wreath, from which depends ribbon suspending 5-pted star (45 bet. points), in centre an acorn on triangle. V. fine. Æ gilt.   1

343 Army of the Potomac. A P in monogram, star above crescent ; below, in centre of a 6-arm cross of gold and red enamel, 35mlm bet. points, crossed cannon serve as a loop, with ribbon depending from crossed swords. ℞ Engraved, 560. Perfect.   1

344 Bergen, Bayonne and Greenville. The Citizens to *Capʔ J. W. Low.* Co C. 21ˢᵗ Regʔ N. J. Vols. — Army of the Potomac, 1862–3 ℞ State arms suptd. Holed, with ring depending from bar, on which a fasces. V. fine and rare. Æ. 34.   1

345 Brooklyn. 1866. Presented by the City — to one of its veterans. A *sailor* stdg in oval. ℞ Female stdg on pedestal, shield shape, with helmet for crest. Loop, ribbon and bar. Fine, very rare. Æ, silvered. 32 x 46.   1

346 Another, from same die as last, with bar and blue velvet ribbon. Perfect, very rare. Æ.   1

347 Another of same design, with *soldier* in oval ; red velvet ribbon. Perfect, rare. Æ.   1

348 Cross with N — G — S — N. Y. ; in centre, a raised circle of blue and red enamel, " Baptized by Fire," and large 14 depending from bar inscribed BROOKLYN ; below hangs the letter F. V. fine. Gold cross, 38 x 28.   1

349 U. S. COLORED | TROOPS. Two negro soldiers charging fort. ℞ Distinguished for courage ; within wreath, Campaign | before | Richmond | 1864 Holed, with ring, to which are attached bar and ribbon. Fine, rare. Æ. 40.   1

350 Grand Army Badge. 5-ptd star, ribbon (a U. S. flag) depending from eagle on cannon. Between pts. 45. Æ. Also miniature of same. Brass. 20. Perfect.   2

351 Star of the Order, outside of which, field is plain. ℞ A star of same proportions, olive branches in the points ; within, the various corps badges. Impression in W.m. from an unfinished die. Perfect, very rare. 50.   1

352 A similar design. Legend, Fraternity — Charity — Loyalty. ℞ Citizens in Peace — in war Soldiers. Perfect proof. Æ. 51.   1

353 Another as last, in W.m. 51. Also a smaller design. ℞ Our Comrades. Soldier placing wreath on tomb. W.m. 38. Proofs.   2

354 Medals commemorating encampments at Baltimore, Denver, Gettysburg and Nashville. Proofs. W.m. 38.   4

355 Others. Baltimore, two types, and Denver. Proofs. Æ. 38.   3

356 Straps (or bars) with ribbons to attach to G. A. R. Badges for National (buff) Department (red) and Post Officers (blue), with the various insignia of rank, from Commander-in-chief down. Buff, 7 ; red, 8 ; blue, 9. Accompanied by a leaf from official communication, giving full explanations. Perfect.   24

357 KEARNEY on sphere in centre of gold cross, 22 x 22, within cir-
     cular band inscribed Dulce et decorum, etc., on black
     enamel. ℞ Engraved in script, 263 | *Lieut. J. D. Schuler* |
     87 *N. Y. V.*, with clasp-pin linked to gold suspender, ribbon
     and long brass pin. Perfect.   1

358 KEARNEY CROSS on scroll in centre of Maltese cross, 42 x 42.
     ℞ BIRNEY'S DIVISION. Ring with ribbon between two sus-
     penders. By *Jacobus, Phila.* V. fine and rare.   1

359 A silver cast of the preceding, with suspenders and ribbon.
     V. fine.   1

THE KEARNEY CROSS. *Gold and Enamel.* "This decoration was adopted at a
meeting of officers representing the regiments which had served under Major-General
Philip Kearney, held in camp near Falmouth, Va., Nov. 29, 1862. Means were care-
fully devised to prevent any one from obtaining or wearing this badge who was not
entitled to display it, in consequence of actual service in battle, under the eyes or leading
of the hero whose motto was to be emblazoned thereon. Only three hundred and
twenty-five officers had received them up to the date when this chapter was prepared."—
*Personal and Military History of Philip Kearney, p. 370, by John Watts DePeyster, New
York, 1869.*

THE MALTESE CROSS. "The Maltese cross for soldiers of Birney's divisions were
ordered by Brigadier-General Birney to present to such of his command as might dis-
tinguish themselves by deeds of valor. Obverse, in a scroll, "Kearney Cross"; on the
reverse, "Birney's Division." One thousand of these were ordered, of which number
five hundred were at once distributed, the remainder reserved for future disposal."—
Ibid., p. 371.

360 MAJ. GEN. KEARNEY | KILLED AT CHANTILLY, above bust *l.* ;
     below, Sept. 1. 1862. ℞ Incuse of obv. with clasping pin.
     V. fine. 27 x 33. Æ.   1

361 Loyal Legion. Gold and blue and white enamelled cross, M.
     O. Loyal Legion, U. S. Fasces in centre on red. ℞ Lex
     Reget. etc. Eagle ; loop, ring and ribbon ; number on ring
     erased, accompanies the button of the Order. Both about
     perfect. Sold as one piece.   1

362 Medical Staff. Gold and green enamelled 5-armed cross,
     45mlm bet. points, in centre 𝕸. 𝕾. on smaller radiated
     silver star. ℞ Engraved in script, *Brevᵗ. Major* | *W. J.
     McDermott* | *Authorized by order of* | *Surgeon Genᵗ. U. S. A.*
     etc. 1865 in 7 lines. Blue ribbon, and suspender held by
     gold eagle, with pin. V. fine, rare.   1

363 Another, as last, with red, white and blue ribbon, 1375 twice
     scratched on rev., otherwise perfect. Rare.   1

364 State of New York, 1865 arms. ℞ Presented to | —— | by
R. C. Fenton | Governor | etc. War of the Rebellion, in 14
lines. About perfect. Æ. 37.   1

365 New York 1865, State arms. ℞ Military — Merit — *Lt. A* —
1865 Engraved, *Lieut* | 𝕿𝖍𝖔𝖘 𝕭. 𝕱𝖎𝖘𝖍 Ring and bar en-
graved C°. O· V. fine, rare. Æ. 34.   1

366 The | State of Ohio | to | (name erased) Veteran | Ohio Vol-
unteer. ℞ Liberty placing wreath on head of soldier. Ex.
1861—1865 Swivel, suspender and ribbon. V. fine. Æ.
37.   1

367 Pittsburgh. 1881. Delegates' badge to annual encampment
Dept. Pa. Ring and bar inscribed Jan | Pittsburgh | 1881
℞ Plain ; shield shape. Perfect. Æ. 30 x 45.   1

368 Another as last. Perfect. Æ.   1

369 Sons of Veterans. VETERANORUM FILII, S V in monogram in
centre, linked to cannon, bar inscribed 1880 | GRATIA DEI
SERVATUS. Perfect. Æ. 35.   1

370 United Veterans. Military trophy. 1861—1865. On cannon,
UNITATE VETERANORUM UNIO. ℞ Plain with border of stars.
Ring with eagle on suspender. Perfect, oval. 34 x 43.
Æ.   1

371 West Virginia. Liberty placing wreath on head of soldier.
1861.—1865. ℞ Presented | by the | State | of | West Vir-
ginia. Swivel ring and bar inscribed HONORABLY DISCHARGED.
Edge, M! Logan C° B 10ᵗʰ Reg. Inf. Vol⁵ Very fine, rare.
Æ. 37.   1

COLUMBUS.

Coins and Medals commemorating the Celebration of 1892–93, *and
others.*

372 Columbia reclining before Administration building, eagle
soaring above, with label, E PLURIBUS UNUM ℞ Bird's-
eye view of Exposition with portions of the city. Ex.,
WORLD'S COLUMBIAN EXPOSITION | CHICAGO 1893. The
largest medal struck for the occasion. By *Lauer.* In
hard Britannia metal, in velvet lined wood case. About
perfect. 115.   1

373 CRISTOFORO COLOMBO Bust ¾ *l.* on concave surface, encircled by America and Europe joining hands under small globe, eagle below. ℞ Allegorical procession of Civilization, surrounded by genii, at sunrise ; group of Indians show concern at its approach ; small shields of the States around border. MCCCCXƆII — MDCCCXƆII. Designed by *Pogliaghi*, executed by *Cappucia*, and published by *Johnson* of Milan. A superb medal, and one of the finest for any occasion. Perfect. Æ. 102.	1

374 CRISTOFORO COLOMBO. Bust in loose robe, holding map. ℞ Figures of Italy and America within Exposition grounds at Genoa, viewing departure of three caravels. Struck for the Italo-American Exposition, Genoa, 1892. Perfect. Aluminum. 90.	1

375 CHRISTOPHER COLUMBUS gave a new world to humanity. Bust *l.* by Tiffany & Co. (*Whitehouse.*) ℞ After | Four Hundred | years of progress | etc. in 6 lines. Wreath with small seal of the Am. Num. and Arch. Soc. Perfect. Æ (gold bronze finish). 77.	1

376 CRISTOBAL COLON etc. Bust *l.* wrapped in mantle. ℞ Su Genio Vislumbro un Mundo etc. Female setd on globe. By *Lauer*. Perfect. Æ. 70.	1

377 CHICAGO 21 . OCTBR. 1892 — Guanahani 12 Octbr. 1492 Columbus in stern of vessel sailing west, guided by Light personified. ℞ Heraldic eagle holds inscribed tablet above Exposition buildings. Published by *Christesen*, Copenhagen. Perfect. Æ. 65.	1

378 Another, from same dies as last. Perfect. W.m. 65.	1

379 IV CENTENARIO DEL DESCUBRIMIENTO DE AMERICA Bust of Columbus ¾ *l.* by *Sneider*. ℞ Venezuela | en la Exposicion | UNIVERSAL | Colombina | de Chicago | 1893 Horse *r.* Perfect. W.m. 61.	1

380 A reduced design of lot 373. Perfect. Æ. 59.	1

381 A similar but larger bust, Memento of Chicago. Another as last. Both W.m. Proof. 59.	2

382 Three caravels sailing around medallion of Columbus. ℞ Spanish and U. S. shields. Inscription in 10 lines. The official medal by the Committee of One Hundred. By *Naegele*. Perfect. Æ and W.m. 57.	2

383 Bare head *l.* in high ruff, by *Lea Ahlborn.* ℞ Scene of his landing on the island which he named San Salvador. Ex., 4 line inscription. Perfect proof. Æ. 51.   1
384 A design similar to 374. Bust within wreath. Genoa Exposition, 1892. Perfect proof. Æ. 50.   1
385 Salvador Republic, 1894. Peso, with bust of Columbus *l.* Fine. Æ. 37.   1
386 Genoa. Same type as lot 374. Perfect. Alumimum. 36.   1
387 Cardenas. ERECCION DE LA ESTATUA DEL INMORTAL COLON etc. Statue of Columbus erected 1862. ℞ Double legend and names of municipal officials, etc., in 16 lines. Perfect, very rare. Brass, oval, 35 x 41. Plate.   1
388 U. S. Columbian Half Dollars, 1892 and 1893. Uncirculated.   2
389 Salvador. 50 Centavos, same type as 385. Very fine. Æ. 31.   1
390 Souvenirs of the 400th anniversary, 2 with ribbon, both alumimum, 2 badges, Æ and B., all with bar; also 1 W.m. All perfect.   5

CONFEDERATE STATES OF AMERICA.

391 1861. Cent. Lib. head *l.* ℞ Value, wreath of southern products. By *Lovett.* V. fine, rare. Æ. 19.   1
392 1861. A UNITED SOUTH Flag *r.* on staff. ℞ Cotton plant. 15 stars around border. Edge plain. Fine, exceedingly rare. Æ. 13. Plate.   1
393 1861. JEFFERSON . DAVIS . Head *l.* by .*C.R.* ℞ CSA FIRST PRESIDENT, date within wreath. Short die-projecting loop, edge milled. Fine, extremely rare. Æ. 18. Plate.   1
394 1861. G. T. BEAUREGARD. BRG. ɢEN. C. S. A. Head *l.* by .*C.R.* ℞ MANASSAS | 21 | JULY | 1861 Olive wreath. Edge milled. V. fine, extremely rare. Æ. 18. Plate.   1
395 1863. Stonewall Jackson. Head *l.* by *Caque.* ℞ Label with names of battles, entwined with wreath, other names in field in 8 lines. Perfect. W.m. 50.   1
396 JACKSON — HOPE MEDAL, the gift of English gentlemen. Military statue of Jackson. By *Koehler.* ℞ Distinguished graduate | Virginia Military | Institute, etc., with labels for inscribing recipient's name. V. fine, very rare. W.m. 50.   1

397 Another, similarly designed, with same legends and inscriptions, without engraver's name.   V. fine and as rare as the
preceding. W.m. 46.   1

398 A rude lead planchet, punched C. S. A. | J. Davis. | Rich-
mond | Va | 1863   ℞ State Rights. — Liberty.   In field
One | 1863 | Cent. | C. S. A.   Good.   40.   1

399 Constitution — 1861.   Scroll.   ℞ Concession | before | Se-
cession.   Æ, Æ, brass, copper, nickel and w.m.   V. choice.
Scarce. 19.   5

400 Obv. impression of Confederate Half Dol.   ℞ 4 Originals,
etc. W.m. Pin.   Eagle on globe with Confed. flag. Brass.
Also eagle with two serpents, on bar having seven stars.
Brass silvered. Fine.   3

400a Electrotype of the Great or Broad Seal of the Confederate
States of America, mounted under glass, in a velvet lined
morocco case, in perfect order; accompanied by a Monograph, giving historical details. 8vo, paper, 23 pp.   Washington, D. C., 1873.   Sold as one piece.   1

COPPER COINS.

401   **Mexico.**   Chas. and Joanna.   Y. F — 4 (2) and F — IIII,
also K. crowned.   ℞ I. crowned.   Poor and fair, rare.   21
to 28.   4

402 1768 C(haˢ) S(pain) linked and crowned, sep. REX — III.
℞ Large M̃ sep. VE (in mon.) — $\frac{1}{16}$.   Fine, very rare. Brass,
21.   1

403 1814–16 $\frac{1}{8}$ (2), $\frac{1}{4}$, $\frac{2}{4}$ (2) Reals.   Two floral F's cwnd. Poor
to good.   5

404 Republic.   1829 $\frac{1}{4}$ Real, large and small; 1830 $\frac{1}{8}$ do. (fair);
1831 $\frac{1}{8}$, $\frac{1}{4}$ do. (2, 1 in brass CS. J. M.); 1834 $\frac{1}{8}$ do. Fine
to unc.   7

405 1842 Lib. setd.   ℞ Octavo | de Real and date, within wrth.;
edge lettered.   Unc.   Mostly red ; rare. 29.   1

406 1843 REPUBLICA MEXICANA.   Eagle on cactus.   ℞ $\frac{1}{8}$ | DE REAL
| 1843 within circle, wrth around border.   Holed near edge,
otherwise very fair.   Extremely rare. 20.   1

407 1863 Centavos of M̃ and S. L. P. mints.   Unc. and fine, scarce.
1868 Ctvo., M̃.   Æ gilt, proof.   Rare.   3

408 States and Cities of Mexico. Campeche. 1861 Centavo. V. good, rare. 21.   1

409 Catorce. 1822 ¼ Real. FONDOS PUBLICOS. ℞ DE CATORCE.
Bird on plant. Good, very rare. 21.   1

410 Chihuahua. 1860 and '66 ¼ Reals. Liberty setd. Very fine.
Colima. 1816 CVART. Fair. 25. 1828 OCT? | DE | COL Gd.
23. Last two rare.   4

411 Compostela. 1856 ⅛ Real. Poor. 29. Cotiga. 1861 ⅛ do.
Bust. ℞ Cwnd arms. Gd, rare. Brass, 20. Hermosillo.
Quartilla, 1835 and '85. Lib. cap. ℞ Arrow bet. quivers.
Fair and good.   4

412 Dolores. PUEBL(O) | DE . LOS | DOLO | RES ℞ Blank. Struck
about 1810, when Hidalgo started the insurrection at this
place. Good, and of the highest rarity. 25.   1

413 Durango. 1816 Fo linked r. and l. with VII in mon. cwnd. ⅛
Real. Good, not well centered, rare. 23.   1

414 1822 ⅛ Real. Arms. ℞ De la | Provincia | de Nueva | Viz-
caya. Fair, ex. rare. 16½. 1823 ¼ do., same design. Good,
rare. 19.   2

415 1828 Octavo. Lib. cap. ℞ Indian with bow and arrow before tree. V. fair, rare. 19.   1

416 1860 (Die varieties), '66 Estado (die varieties) and " Depart-
amento." All ¼ Reals. Fair to good. 27.   5

417 1872 ¼ Real, "Sufragio Libre." Eagle. ℞ Wreath, value,
date. Good, v. rare. 26.   1

418 Guanajuato. 1829 Octavo, good. 20. Cuartilla, poor. 27.
Both rare.   2

419 Jalisco. 1862 Octavo. Bow, arrow, quiver and flag. Good.
28. Merida de Yucatan, 1856 ½ Grano de Peso. Very
good. 26. 1876 Similar type, poor. The last two in
lead.   3

420 Mazatlan. ADMITIDO—EN MAZATLAN (Received in Mazatlan).
A circular CS., 9 mlm., on otherwise plain planchet, 22 mlm.
Fine, very rare.   1

421 *Mesquite* A tree. ℞ Small rosette in centre. Good, rare.
22.   1

422 Morelia. 1837 ⅛ Real. Indian stdg l., bet. branches, holds
a lib. cap on pole. ℞ MUNICIPALIDAD DE MORELIA. Gd,
very rare. Brass, 28.   1

423 Motul. 1878 ⅛ Real. CIUDAD DDE MOTUL ℞ Value and
date. Fair, rare. Lead, 22.   1

424 San Luis Potosi. 1830 and '67 Dif. types of ¼ Reals. Sinaloa.
¼ Reals, 1861, '62, '66. Sonora. 1859 Cuartilla. Good to
fine. 26½ to 32.   6

425 San Felipe. VILLA DE SAN FELIPE. Cross within a dotted
circle. 31. Another, S. FE | LIPE | NERI 29. Blank re-
verses. Good, rare.   2

426 UNION in monogram. ℞ Plain. Temax. 1872 ⅛ Real. VILLA
DE TEMAX. Tixkokob. 1877 Octavo. AYUNTA? DE TIXKOKOB.
Fair, rare. Lead, 20 to 27.   3

427 Yxtlan. 1853 ¼ Real, 2 var. (1 holed). Poor. 21. Zacatecas.
1862, '63 Octavos and Quartillas. Fine. Brass, 22, 28.
Zamora. Octavos, CS. z^ also z^ and ⅛. Good. Brass, 22.
Also ¼ above bird r. ℞ Plain. Unknown. Good.
21.   9

428 **West Indies.** St. Eustatius. S E. CS on Cayenne Sou.
Another similar, with P subsequently stamped. Good.   2

429 San Domingo. Ferd. VII, ¼ Real, F. 7. cwnd. ℞ Value and
S. D. 26. Tobago. T B stamped on Cayenne Sou. 23.
Good.   2

430 Varieties of last lot, with 2 of Tobago. Good.   3

431 **So. America.** Am | de . La | Cuadra, 1855. Caracas. ⅛
Real, 1818 (rare) ; ¼ do., 1816, '17, '18, '21. Good to fine.
20 to 28.   6

432 Carthagena. 1812 ½ Real (2 var.) ; 1813 2 Rls. Indian setd
under tree beside cabin. Rude coinage. Fine. 20, 22,
29.   3

433 Cayenne. 1789–1816, 1848 Sou to 10 Ctms. Billon. Espi-
nosa, Mitad. 29. Sancarlo, ¾ Rl. 28. All fine.   6

434 Peru. 1822 ¼ Real. Provisional. ℞ Sun in rays. Rare. 16.
Santa Marta. F. VII | 1813. ℞ Large S. M. Rare. 20.
1820 ¼ Rl. S M and cross. 20. All fine.   3

435 Var. of last 2 pcs, dates not good. Velez, Mitad. Fine. 29.
Span. Guiana. Ferd. VII, ½ Real, 1813, '14, '15. Good.
24 to 29.   6

436 Suriname. 1679 2 and 4 Doits. Parrot on branch. 1764
Doit. Coffee plant. Good to fine. 19, 20, 21.   3

HACIENDA AND MERCHANTS' TOKENS.

437 **Mexico.** Ahnacatlan. E. Partida, $\frac{1}{8}$, $\frac{1}{4}$ Rl. Ameca. 1802, '06 Monograms; 1826 $\frac{1}{4}$ Rl.; 1853, '55 $\frac{1}{8}$ do. by V. F. Hacienda Del Carmen; 1877 $\frac{1}{8}$, $\frac{1}{4}$ do. Campania. B. F. Autlan, 1855 $\frac{1}{8}$ do. Fair to fine. Æ and brass, 20 to 26.   10

438 Guadalaxara. M. Alvarez, 1873 Ctvo. A beehive. T. C., n.d. Los Angeles. M. Yingo, $\frac{1}{4}$ and 1 Rl. Mineral de Guadalupe, mon. 1845 $\frac{1}{4}$ Rl. (type of coinage 1829–36). Good to fine. Æ, brass and iron, 18$\frac{1}{2}$ to 25.   5

439 Montero. J. A. Lardaeta, 1866 $\frac{1}{4}$ Real. Scales. ℞ Value, date in wreath. Fon. 6932. Fine. Nickel, 20.   1

440 Motul. S. T. L(eon), $\frac{1}{8}$ Real. J(ose) G(onzales), n.d. Both lead, plain rev. Sta. Elena. D(esiderio) L(izarraga), mon. Brass. Also 2 Reals by Santiago Fernandes. Brass. Good. 23 to 30.   4

441 Orizaba. Hac. del Jazmin. ℞ A. E. J. in mon. Quezaltenango. Tahea Pacheco, Fon. 7290. San Gabriel. M. Hermanos, 1 Rl. San Jose Kuche. J. Ancona E Hijos, 1874 2$\frac{1}{2}$ Ctvs. Fon. 8293. Santo Tomas. J. H. C., mon., 1875, 2 Rls. Fine. Brass, 18 to 30.   5

442 Temax. E. N. P(erez), 1881 $\frac{1}{4}$ Rl. ℞ Plain (lead). Tepec. Bonizacia Peña, $\frac{1}{8}$ Rl. Hac. de Puga, 1871 6$\frac{1}{4}$ Ctvs. (2 var.) San Blas, 5 Ctvs. Loreto Corona, 1858 $\frac{1}{8}$ Rl. Poor to good. Æ and brass, 21 to 30.   6

443 Tequila. L. J. Gallado, 1857 Octavos (3), type 2 trees, and Quartilla, demijohn bet. casks; 3 are CS with dog, horse or eagle. Good to fine. Æ and brass, 20 to 28.   4

444 Tuxpango, Hacienda de, 5 and 10 Ctvs. ℞ The Mexican eagle. Fine. Brass, 26, 30.   2

445 Vera Cruz. R. Sierra y H'no, 1881 $\frac{1}{4}$ Rl. Yerrere, $\frac{1}{8}$ and $\frac{1}{4}$ do. (rude brands), M. R. and M. P. Both monograms, with others, unknown. Poor to fine. 14 to 34.   9

446 VALE | OS NEGOCꜱ DE G. L. for 20, 60 (2) and 140 (?) ℞ Plain. Good. Lead. 24 to 31.   4

447 BUTRON | Y | MUXICA. ℞ Ano | de | 1806 Good. Brass, 32. BLANCO above serpent coiled around chalice. ℞ Cuartillo above cactus plant. Fine. Brass, 27.   2

448   CAS | TRO, MON | NOS etc. 2 with Mex. eagle ; odd shapes, only 1 round ; all with blank revs. Fine. 16 to 23.   5

449   **Central America.**   Antigua, Guatemala (M.M.) Herrara, 1871. Fon. 7289. Bluefields, S. Parsons, 1878, 2½ Cts. Cerrillos, ½ Rl., by V. N., 1864. Fon. 7471. Corozal, A. A. V. and E. T. B. Costa-Rica, F. Giralt. Honduras, Zelay I. Diaz, 1877, 10 Ctvs. San Jose, Nanne & Aguilar. Fon. 7366. San Ysidro, 1877, ½ Rl., by J. A. C. Fine to unc. Æ, brass and lead, 17 to 22.   9

450   **West Indies.**   Cuba. Havana, Nogues y Lafitte, located at O'Reilly, 13. ℞ Vessel approaching the island. Fine. Brass, 28.   1

451   Matanzas, Labayen y Hermano. A padlock. ℞ Steamer Leviathan. Fon. 7745. Unc. W.m. 32.   1

452   Haiti. Port au Prince. ℞ A. T. | & | B. R. within wreath. Fine. W.m. 27.   1

453   **So. America.**   Callao, "The Club," 1867, 2 Reals, nickel. Juan Lapeyre, 1863, ½ Rl. Schmidt, 1 Rl (holed). Isla de Chincha-Qumlin, Medio Real. Good to fine. All rare. 19 to 24.   4

454   Canete, H. Swayne, ½ Real. 18. Colon, Coll Brandon & Co., 2½ Cts. ℞ Train of cars and palm-tree. Brass, nearly proof. 27. Caracas, B. Bonfanti & Co., ½, 1, 2 Rls., nickel. Unc. 15, 18, 22½.   5

455   Carabobo, B. Antich, 1881, 1 Rl. Carthagena, Manuel Mª P., 1838, Mitad (struck over Merchants' Ex., 1837 token). Fon. 8199. Yngenio Ecuador, M. & J. F. De la Vega, 1864, 1 Rl. (4 metals.) Fon. 8326. Esquina del Verde, M. Angulo, device a cannon. Good to unc. 19 to 29.   7

456   Copane. F B in script. Medaglie del Iappalto. ℞ Copane in circolazione. A basket. Good, very rare. Iron, 29.   1

457   Cochabamba. Nicasio de Gumucio, 1876, 5 Ctvs. Lion beneath tree. Fine, unc. Æ 15½.   1

458   Lima. Americano and Morin's Hotel, 1859; D. Barraza and D. J. De Castro, both 1858. All ½ Reals. Fine. 19, 20.   4

459   Mompos, R. Hermanos, 2½ Ctvs. Serpent, club and bowl. Fon. 8215. Fair, rare. Brass, 30.   1

460   José M. Ruis, 1844, Mitad. ℞ Face of sun in rays. Fine work, with broad milled borders. V. fine, rare. 29.   1

461   Montalban, A. Perez, 1857, and H. Munoz, 1864, both with
cock *l.* Santander, E. R. C. and without name, 1874. Son-
sonate, J. Mathe, oblongs, length 55, 4 widths, stamped letters. All fine and brass.   8

462   Tacna, A. Bertelon, Quartillo. Urachiche, Z. Antich, 1858,
¼, ½ Rl. Yaracuy, J. B. Hellyer, 1858, Rl. Zambrano, A.
A. de Hoyos, Mitad (oval). Others, Compania del Senu
(2), etc. Good to unc. ; most of last, 1 in tin. 10 to 25.   10

SILVER COINS.

463   **Mexico.** Chas. and Joanna. Large K I cwnd, P-LV-S through
pillars in sea. M-O-I Good. P(?)-M-O Poor, holed. Half
Rls. 21.   2

464   Cwnd arms. ℞ Pillars. 1 Real. L-M̂ 2 do. G-M and M-S.
V. fair to v. good. 23 to 28.   3

465   2 Reals, L-M. Nearly fine, 28. Another, M̂-M̂ with PLVS in
frame through columns, G below. V. fair, holed, rare. 27.   2

466   4 Reals, type as 464, L-M̂. Fine, rare. 31.   1

467   Phil. II and III, ½, 1 and 2 Rls. Poor to v. fine, 2 holed. 12
to 28.   6

468   2 Reals, PHLIPVS · REI · DELAS ' 791 ' Cwnd arms, M-M HIS-
PANIARUM ' SO ' REX ' DE ' LAS ' IND + ℞ Arms of Castile
and Leon in angles of cross. Holed, otherwise very good.
Possibly a contemporary counterfeit. 27.   1

469   Phil. III, 1671, 8 Rls. M̂ | D-8 Cwnd arms. ℞ ISPANIARVM ·
ET ' IN ' DIARVM ' REX ' Type as last. Fine, though thrice
holed. 46.   1

470   Phil. V, 1721, '22, ½ Rls. Mon. cwnd. Good, both holed.
¼ Rls, 1807, '08, '09, (holed); '10, '13, and 2 without date or
value. *Obv.,* castle ; *rev.,* lion. Fair to unc.   8

471   Chas. IV, 1808, 8 Rls. Bust type. M̂· 8R· T. H. Fine. 39.   1

472   Ferd. VII, 1809, 8 Rls. Type and marks as last ; slight
marks of circulation. 39.   1

473   1821, ½, 1, 2 and 4 Rls. All M̂. J. J., in mint state ; a very rare
condition.   4

474   1821, 8 Rls., Zacatecas mint. Z⸱ 8R. R. G. V. fine. 38.   1

475   Augustin (Iturbide), 1822, ½, 1 and 2 Rls, in mint state ; an
extremely rare condition.   3

476 1822, 8 Rls. AUGUST · DEI · PROV · Small head, long neck
     and bust. ℞ Small eagle, head *l.* Slight marks of circula-
     tion on rev., otherwise brilliant, approaching proof. Very
     rare.   1

477 1822. 8 Rls. Large head, legend as last. ℞ Eagle's head
     r. Very good. 39.   1

478 1822. 8 Rls. Head sim. to last. AUGUSTINUS DEI PROVIDEN-
     TIA V. fine. 39.   1

479 1822. 8 Rls. Sim. IMPERATOR above eagle. Very fine.
     39.   1

480 1823. ½ and 2 Rls. Mint state, very rare. 17, 26.   2

481 1823. 8 Rls. Smallest bust, and not pointed, otherwise same
     variety as 479. Good. 39.   1

482 Republic, 1823. 8 Rls. Liberty cap on rays. ℞ Eagle *l.*
     "Hook-neck Dollar," ᴍ̃. Good. 38.   1

483 1824. 8 Rls, same type differently executed. D° mint. V.
     good. 39.   1

484 1824. 8 Rls, same type. ᴍ̃ mint. V. fine. 37½.   1

485 1824. 8 Rls, same type. G° mint. Fine, rare. 39½.   1

486 1825. 8 Rls, as last. Nearly fine, rare. 40.   1

487 1826. REPUBLICA MEXICANA. Field plain. ℞ LIBERTAD and
     14 stars around border. In field, a rosette. Fine, very
     rare. 21.   1

488 1862. 8 Rls. Lib. cap and rays. ℞ Eagle erect, head *r.* ᴍ̃
     mint. Fine. 38.   1

489 1862. 8 Rls. Oaxaca mint. Good. 38.   1

490 1862. 8 Rls. Z° mint. A wheel CS. on Liberty cap. Very
     good. 38.   1

491 1863. 2 Rls, ᴍ̃. 8 do., G° Uncirculated. 27½, 39.   2

492 1866. 8 Rls. H° mint. V. good. 39.   1

493 1867. 8 Rls. Culiacan, Oaxaca and (San Luis) Potosi mints.
     Fine to v. fine.   3

494 CANTON DE TUXTLA, 1861. ¼ Rl. ℞ Eagle. Good, very rare.
     12.   1

495 Mexican eagle in circle on 1 Rl, in oval also on 2 do., both
     CS. Good, rare.   2

496 Another pair as last, but from dif. dies. Good.   2

497 M C and T S A (in mon.) CS on cut halves of ½ Real pcs.
     Fine.   2

498 **Central America, etc.** Guatemala. 1812 Med. 2 Rls. Sept. 24th. Arms. ℞ Open book on rays. Fon. 7195, Fis. 13. V. fine, brill. 27. Also 1818, '21, and Nicaragua, 1803, '16, ¼ Rls. Castle and Lion type. Good to unc. 11, 12.   5

499 Curacoa. ¼ Gulden. C in script CS on ¼ Holland Guld. Edges have 16 crenations. Fine.   1

500 St. Lucia. s LUCIE CS on ⅛ of M̃8 Rls. Good, rare.   1

501 **South America.** Caracas. 1818, 2 Rls. LV–SVL–TR 1819, do., Plv–svl–tr 1820, do., Plv–slv–tra. Usual type, 2 with F–7. Good. 24.   3

502 Bolivia. 1865, ½ Rl. Hd of Melgarejo *l.* ℞ Winged dragon. Fon. 9682. 15. Real, Beehive. ℞ Mil. trophy. Fon. 9667. 18. Both fine. Potosi, 1808. Santiago, 1817. ¼ Rls. Castle and Lion type. Good. 12.   4

503 Santiago. · VINCIT · LABOR · · OMNIA · IMPROBA · · Bust of Chas. IV *r.*, laur. and mailed. ℞ · HISPAN · ET · IND · REX · S · B · DE · PLA · Cwnd arms bet. pillars. Fine. 40.   1

Centre of obverse has an oval link (in die), indicating place for shank, such as commonly found on imitation coins designed for equestrian ornaments; but this is in good silver and bears the general type of the 8 Real pieces.

504 **Cob Money.** Mexico. Phil. II, 2 (holed), 4 and 8 Rls. Poor and fair.   3

505 Others, 2 and 8 Rls, the latter CS with Golden Fleece. Phil. V, 1733, 8 Rls, holed. Poor and fair.   3

506 Potosi. Chas. II, (16)94 and '99, 2 Rls. Phil. V, 1727, 8 do., holed. Poor and fair.   3

507 1, 2 and 4 Rls, 1757–64. The first named is rare. Fair.   3

508 8 Rls. Poor, prob. Potosi. 2 do., various, 1724–1755; one differing from usual type, has circular CS. Fair.   8

PROVISIONAL COINS OF MEXICO.

REVOLUTIONARY PERIOD, 1810–15.

Silver, excepting 509 and 514.

509 ¼ Real, Lion; ¾ do. cwnd arms, with date. Good. 16, 21.   2

510 Ferd. VII, 1 and 2 Rls. Bust *r.*, sep. F—7. ℞ Cwnd arms, sep. 1—R. Same type, 2—R. (clipped.) Very fair, very rare. 18, 25.   2

511 DEPOSIT. D. L. AUTORID. D. F. 7 on mantle. ℞ AMERICANO
        CONGRESO. Eagle on cactus, sep. 1—R. Good, very rare.
        20.   1

512 1811. 8 Rls. FERDIN · VII · DEI · GRATIA 1811   Eagle on cac-
        tus, above oval arched bridge, sep. 8—R. ℞ PROUICIONAL ·
        POR · LA · SUPREMA · JUNTA DE AMERICA ·   Halberd and
        quiver crossed ; above, hand holds bow and arrow ; below, a
        lasso. Original cast. Fon. 6496. Good, very rare. 35½.   1

513 1812. ½ Real. VICE FERD. VII . DEI . GRATIA . ET . ℞ S. P.
        CONG. NAT. IND. GUV. T. S. M. Device same as preceding.
        Fon. 6504. Good, but holed. 17. Same type Real, with
        GUV. T. 1 R. S. M. Fis. 151, Fon. 6503. 20. V. fair ; both
        rare.   2

514 1812. 2 Rls. Same type, with legends (abbreviated), same as
        512. Fis. 150. Barely fair. Æ. 29.   1

515 1812. 8 Rls. Same type as 513, with GUV. T. 8 R. S. M̊. Fis.
        152. Fon. 6501. Fine, extremely rare. 39.   1

516 1813. ½ Real. Type of 513, differently executed. S. J. N. G.
        DEI . GRATIA ℞ GUV. T. M̊. S. M. etc. Very fair, extremely
        rare. 18.   1

517 1813. 4 Rls. Type of 513, with 4 R. S. M̊. V. fine, some parts
        weakly struck ; a denomination not in Fis. or Fon. Ex-
        tremely rare. 35.   1

518 1813. 8 Rls. Type of preceding ; not in Fis. or Fon. Very
        fair, very rare. 39.   1

519 **Nueva Viscaya.** Ferd. VII (1811), 8 Rls. Spanish arms.
        ℞ (Mon.) PROV. (de) NVEV. VISCA(YA) Arms of the Prov-
        ince. Fon. 6776. Very rare ; poor, though I never saw a
        better one. 39.   1

520 **Oaxaca.** Ferd. VII, 1812. 1 Real. Castle, lion and F. 7.
        in the angles of a cross ; border of dots. ℞ 1 R M PROV. D.
        OAXACA . 1812 Lion *l.* in plain shld. An original cast, as
        are also the two following ; not in Fis. or Fon. Fine, ex-
        tremely rare. 20. Plate.   1

521 1812. 8 Rls. Same type. I°I cwnd, CS on obv. ℞ Shield
        has border with 8 crosses, and lion is *r.* CS c. Border of
        dots obv. and rev. Fine, extremely rare. 3S. Plate.   1

522 1812. 8 Rls. As last, with Z. for rev. CS. Fine, extremely
        rare. 39. Plate.   1

523 **Sombrerete.** Ferd. VII. 1812. ½ Real. (Ferdin.) VII.
SOMBRER(ETE) Cwn above two globes. ℞ VARGAS Small
shld, sep. ½—(R) ; below, (181)2. Not in Fis. or Fon. Fair,
extremely rare. 17.   1

524 1811. 8 Rls. (R. Caxa) DE SOMB(RETE) Arms. ℞ CS VAR-
GAS | ISI— 1811—ISI | 3. Obv. poor, rev. good. 38.   1

525 1812. 4 Rls. Sim., though better designed, with rev. from a
die. Fon. 7076. Poor, extremely rare. 34.   1

526 1812. 8 Rls. As last. CS on obv., L. V. S. in oblong frame,
with border of stars. Good, an unusual condition. Rare.
38.   1

527 **Zacatecas.** Ferd. VII, 1810. ½ Real. Spanish arms. ℞
MONEDA PROVISIONAL DE ZACATECAS. Mountain, L. V. O.
and 7 stars below. Not in Fis. or Fon. A very rare date
and denomination. Obv. good, rev. poor. 16.   1

528 1811. 2 Rls. Similar, with 2 mountains and 19 stars.
Good, rev. not well centered. 25.   1

529 1811. 2 Rls. as last. CS on rev., with eagle on cactus
above oval arched bridge. 16 mlm. Poor and holed, yet
extremely rare. 27.   1

530 1811. 8 Rls. Same type as 528, with 20 stars. Fine. Rare
so choice. 39.   1

531 1811. 2 Rls. Sim. to 528, differently executed. FERDIN. VII.
2–R. DEI etc., and date in legend. 10 stars below L. V. O.
Good. 27.   1

532 1811. 8 Rls. Sim. Obv. fair, rev. *very* poor, holed. 40.   1

533 1812. 8 Rls. Bust *r.* ℞ Cwnd arms, date on both sides.   1
A rare provisional issue, poor, but seldom found better. 38.   1

COINAGE OF THE MEXICAN REVOLUTIONARY GENERAL,
JOSE MARIA MORELOS.

The copper pieces in this magnificent collection are chiefly from the find of Morelos
coins which formed the basis of my paper before the Am. Num. and Arch. Soc'y in 1886.
Much of the silver is from the collection of the late Father Fischer, a catalogue of which
was published by the Scott Stamp and Coin Co., in 1891. There are no duplicates,
although the die varieties are quite extensive.

COPPER.

534 1811. 2 Rls. Monogram of Morelos | .2. R. | 1811. ℞ SUD.
beneath bow and arrow, type of all following. A very rare
date. Good. 21.   1

535 1812. 1 Real. Good, very rare. 20.   1
536 1812. 1, 2 and 8 Reals. Fair to good. 20, 24, 34.   3
537 1812. 2 Reals. Smallest bow; varieties, one with two periods
        after SUD. V. good. 22 to 26.   4
538 1812. 2 Rls. Varieties, S reversed, period before SUD,
        punctuated date, etc. Fair to v. good. 21 to 24.   4
539 1812. 2 Rls. Varieties. Bow-string and arrow feathered,
        arrow-foot below bow-string, etc. Fair to good. 21 to 29.   4
540 1812. 2 Rls. Varieties. Feathered arrow, straight top bow,
        * 2 * R etc. Fair to good. 20 to 25.   4
541 1812. 2 Rls. Varieties. Large bow, feathered arrow; coarse
        milling, etc. Fair to good. 24 to 27.   4
542 1812. 2 Rls. Varieties. Long low bow, 2 with dots inside
        of bow, small and medium dates. Good. Another with
        Morelos monogram CS on rev. Poor but very rare. 24
        to 27.   4
543 1812. 8 Rls. Short feathered bow-string, without periods or
        punctuations. Good. 37.   1
544 1812. 8 Rls. Feathered bow-string, periods, etc. P and a
        small s reversed form the letter R. V. good. 38.   1
545 1812. 8 Rls. Arrow bet. minute dots within bow. Broad and
        wide milling, small date. Fine. 38.   1
546 1812. 8 Rls. One sim. to last. Good. 36. Another with
        feathered bow-string. CS on rev. with mon. and star. Fair,
        and a cast of the following lot. Poor. 36, 37.   3
547 1812. 8 Rls. Border formed by a dot and dash alternating.
        CS as last. Very good, rare. 39.   1
548 1812. 2 and 8 Rls, with monogram bet. 2—R. Good; rare
        variety. 22, 33.   2
549 1812. 2 and 8 Rls. Bow with straight top, connecting two
        curves; feathered arrow, below bow-string. 2 R, fair; 8 R,
        good. 26, 35.   2
550 1812. 2 and 8 Rls. Borders of dots and line of same below
        bow. Very rare variety. Good. 27, 37.   2
551 1812. 2 and 8 Rls. Bow in semi-circle. Fair and good. 26,
        35.   2
552 1812. 8 Rls. Traces of milling on obv., floral attempt for
        border of rev., feathered bow string and SUD. V. fair.
        Rare. 36.   1

553 1812. 2 Rls. (2 var., 1 struck over a piece inscribed A | HO Low XIII) and 8 Rls. All with floral designs on obv. and rev. Fair to v. good. 24, 26, 34.   3

554 1813. 2 Rls. Round top 3, small and medium SUD, milled borders. Fair and good. 23, 24.   3

555 1813 2 Rls. Varieties. Straight and curved bowstring, and without dot bet. 2 and R. Good to fair. 24, 25.   3

556 1813. 2 Rls. With the remarkable date 18813. Good. 25.   1

557 1813. 8 Rls. Milled borders, arrow bet. 2 small dots within bow; 8 distant from R; a bold impression, excepting borders. 38.   1

558 1813. 8 Rls. Sim., 8 in date very low, heavy bow, without dot inside. Good. 37.   1

559 1813. 8 Rls. Small monogram, the two parts of top equally oval (the right is usually pointed); feathered bow-string. V. good. 37.   1

560 1813. 8 Rls. Sim. to last; row of dots, *l.* parallel with arrow. CS on ob., with Morelos mon. Good. 37.   1

561 1813. Another, with distinguishing features. CS as last. V. good. 39.   1

562 1813. 8 Rls. Coarse representations of roses and leaves. ℞ 2 long leaves encircle bow and arrow; roses with stems, below SUD. Round top 3 (all that follow are square). Fine.   1

563 1813. 8 Rls. With and without period after date; punctuations very large. V. good. 34, 35.   2

564 1813. 8 Rls. Straight top bow, varying monogram and other differing details. Good and v. good. 34 to 36.   3

565 1813. 2 Rls. Type of preceding, with ★ T ★ C ★ | ★ SUD ★ Probably for the Tierra Caliente (warm lands). Stars for punctuations. Borders of nopal leaf and star alternating. V. good and rare. 23.   1

566 1813. 8 Rls. Type of preceding. Fine, rare. 39. Plate.   1

567 1814. 8 Rls. Type of 562. Fine and very rare. 35. Plate.   1

568 1814. 8 Rls. Same general type. ℞ SUD. | · O . X . A · V. fair and extremely rare. I do not know of its duplicate. 37. Plate.   1

569 Various. 1812, '13, '14. 2 Rls (2) and 8 do. (4). Poor and fair.   6

SILVER.

In the following lots, 570–584 inclusive, 570, 571, 578, and 581 are struck from dies; the remainder are original casts.

570 ✓ 1811. 8 Rls. Closely resembling 562. Very good, extremely rare. 38.   1

571 ✓ 1812. 2 Rls. Type of 534. Milled borders, distant from edge. Fis. 496. V. good. 25. Plate.   1

572 1812. 2 Rls. Type of 562. Tulips and roses on obv. Fis. 497, Fon. 6936. Fine. 27.   1

573 1812. 8 Rls. Sim. to 562. Roses larger and better defined. Fis. 498. Fine and very rare. 37½.   1

574 18·12. 8 Rls. Punctuated date. Sim. to 572 ; broad, close milled borders. Fine, rare. 40.   1

575 1813. Half Real. M. | M R. | 1813. ℞ SUD. Bow and arrow. Borders of leaves. Fon. 6946. Fine, very rare. 16.   1

576 1813. Real. Similar. Two leaves nearly encircle bow and arrow. Not in Fis. or Fon. Fine, very rare. 20.   1

577 1813. Real. Similar to last, but with Morelos' mon. instead of plain M. and round-top 3. Fis. 514, Fon. 6945. Good, holed. 19.   1

578 ʽ 1813. Half Real. AMERICA MORELOS Lion *l.* ℞ PROVICIONAL DE OAXACA Fis. 513, Fon. 6948. Clipped and holed, otherwise v. fair. 17. Plate.   1

579 1813. 8 Rls. Very similar to 574. Fon. 6939. Fine, rare. 41.   1

580 18·13. 8 Rls. Sim. to last ; milling coarse and not as deep ; date punctuated. Fine, rare. 40.   1

581 ✓ 1814. Real. Morelos' mon. beneath date. ℞ · v · I · R · Wrth around borders. Found in the Fis. collection only. Good, holed, extremely rare. 16½. Plate.   1

582 **Wooden Money. Huatusco** | año de 1846 in oblong frame. Fine oblong octagon, 32 x 45. Very rare.   1

583 Tlascala (near the city of Mexico). Script Monogram of Tlascala. ℞ 1876. Good, very rare. 38.   1

584 YOANTLA around border. In field (1) 863. Good, very rare. 39.   1

MEDALS OF MEXICO.

Æ. Silver.   Æ. Copper.

585 Charles III. 1778 ✻ CARLOS ✻ III ✻ PADRE ✻ DE ✻ LA ✻ PATRIA ✻ etc. Bust in armor *r.* ✻ VENCE ✻Y TRIUNFA ✻ etc. ℞ Mars setd. at table on elevation, with four others in attendance, below a setd. figure *r.* another standing at *l.* By *G. A. Gil.* Not in Her. or Fon. Fine, very rare. Æ. 58.   1

586 1778. Another from same dies as last. Fis. 74. Fine. Æ. 58.   1

587 1785. Busts of Chas. III. *r.*, Chas. IV and wife *l.*, below infant Ferd. VII *l.* ℞ ✻ IAM ✻ NOVA ✻ PROGENIES ✻ etc. Scene at mine shaft, miners, etc. By *A. Gil.* Fon. 6394. Holed, otherwise good. Scarce. Æ. 62.   1

588 1788. Bust *r.* wearing Order of Golden Fleece. ✻ MEXICANA ✻ ✻ ACADEMICA ✻ FUNDATORI ✻ SUO ✻ etc. By *G. A. Gil.* ℞ ✻ QUI ✻ INGENUAS ✻ etc. A tomb. By *G. Gil.* Type Fis. 81, Fon. 6398. V. fine, brilliant, a few light scratches. Rare. Æ. 65.   1

589 CARLOS III . DE ESP. EMP . DE LAS INDIAS. Bust *r.*, laur. By *Gironimo · A · Gil ·* ℞ AL MERITO. Fine ; a few sm. nicks. Very rare. Æ. 55.   1

590 Charles IV. MARIA † LUISA † REINA † etc. 1793. Bust by *Gil.* ℞ DISTINGUE ✻ PREMIA ✻ etc. The queen distributing insignia of the Order founded in her name in 1792. Lettered edge. Fon. 6426, type Fis. 101. V. fine. Æ. 55.   1

591 1796. Busts of the King and Queen conjoined *r.*, by *Gil.* CARLOS ✻ IV ✻ PIO ✻ BENEF ✻ etc. Equestrian statue. Fis. 105, Fon. 6436. Fine. Æ. 59.   1

592 1796. Another, same design as last. Fis. 106, Fon. 6437. V. fine. Æ. 33½.   1

593 1802. DEDICADA A LA REAL ACADEMIA DE (mon.) S. CARLOS. Art personified, stdg. Ex. F. GORDILLO INVENTO . Y | GRABO · EN Ñ · 1802. ℞ Incuse of obv. From Fis. cat. 112, and I do not know of another. Thin. V. fine. Æ. 38.   1

594 Ferd. VII. 1808. PADRE · DE UN PUEBLO · LIBRE · etc. Bust *r.*, below TOMAS SVRIA ℞ SIEMPRE FIELES · etc. Three hands clasped on spear within radiation, crown above, below, eagle, lion, flags, etc. Fon. 6744, Fis. type 132. About perfect. Æ. 51.   1

595 1809. TODO RENACE Three Generals setd at table on ros-
trum, below, A LA INMORTALIDAD | etc. in 6 lines. ℞ RES-
TAURADORA DE LA EUROPA. Mexico stdg before bags of
money, offering to Mars who holds shield, below, UN AMERI-
CANO etc. in 5 lines. Type Fis. 133, Fon. 6485. Very fine,
a few nicks at edge. Æ. 51.   1

596 1809. FERDIN. VII · etc. Bust *l*. ℞ FIDELITAS DOLI etc. Female carrying portrait of Ferd. VII to temple *l*. Ex., ins. in
3 lines. Die projecting ornament with loop. Fis. 137, Fon.
6483. Fine, though many small nicks. Æ gilt, oval.
47 x 53.   1

597 1809. AMADO FERNANDO VII · etc. Bust *r*. ℞ LA INDUSTRI
Y EL UALOR (*sic*) etc. Mars and Mercury stdg. Fis. 139,
Fon. 6484. V. fine, a few light nicks. Die projecting loop
with palms. Æ gilt, oval. 45 x 53.   1

598 1812. CONSTITUCION POLITICA etc. Open book, cwnd. ℞
Antonio | Bergosa, Arzo- | bispo etc. Fis. 149, Fon. 6500.
Unc., brill. Æ. 28.   1

599 1814. Ferd. VII. Bust *r*., legend in small letters. ℞ SUB
CLIPEO etc. Mercury returning with flag of the Consulate.
Fis. 164; not in Her. or Fon. Nearly perfect. Æ. 51.   1

600 1814. SUBACTA PERFIDIA etc. Ferd. setd on throne. ℞ Fer-
dinando | optimo regi | solio restituto | capitulum | Eccles ·
Mexic · | 1814 Fis. 162, Fon. type 6511. Very fine. Æ.
52.   1

601 1817. Conjoined busts of Ferd. VII and Maria Elisab. *r*.
By *Gordillo*. ℞ FAUSTO SANCTOQUE etc. Two hearts on
pedestal bearing arms of Spain and Portugal, crown above.
Fis. 172; not in Her. or Fon. About perfect. Æ. 42.   1

602 1820. Premio Adquirido en Euestud? Academ.º de Prof.ºr ex-
amin.d.º y examin.ºr D. Jose . Ign.º Paz. Busts of Ferd. and
wife in small oval on pillars ins. Plus Ultra ; behind, fort and
open sea. By *Gordillo* 1818. ℞ AL FELIZ CUMPLEANOS | DE
NUESTRO ADORADO | etc. 1820, in 9 lines. Die proj. loop.
Fis. 178; not in Her. or Fon. Very fine and rare. Æ.
Oval. 39 x 45. Plate.   1

603 FERNANDO VII . REY etc. Bust *l*. ℞ EN | PREMIO DE LA |
FIDELIDAD. Wreath, loop and ring. Fis. 183, Fon. 6468.
V. fine. Æ gilt. 38.   1

604 FERNANDO 7º. ℞ SO A 12 DERECHA. Legend in large letters, original hole in centre, 12 mlm. Probably a military medal. Good. Æ. 35. 1

605 Regency. 1821–22. Military Medal. SPONSIONE TRIPLICI ✶ ORBEM AB ORBE SOLVIT. Three rings linked above 2 globes, severed chain. ℞ PRIMA EPOCHA above wreath of stems, die proj. loop. Fon. 6534. V. fine and rare. Æ. 49. 1

606 Another, sim. CON LA TRIPLE GARANTIA ✶ — DESATO A UN ORBE DE EL OTRO ℞ PRIMERA EPOCA · Fis. 185, Fon. 6535. Fine. Æ. 50. 1

1821.

607 Augustin. PRO RELIGIONE ET PATRIA. Iturbide receives sword from Mexico. ℞ AVGVSTINO . DE ITURBIDE etc. in 4 lines, on mantle draped from bow, on which an eagle. Not in Fis. or Fon. About perfect. Æ. 56. 1

608 MEJICO | EN LA SOLEMNE | etc. in 7 lines. Eagle on cactus plant. Fis. 186, Fon. 6535. V. fine, brilliant. Æ. 34. 1

1822.

609 INAUGURACION | DE AGUSTIN . | etc. in 5 lines. ℞ Sim. design to last. Fis. 188, Fon. 3539. V. fine. Æ. 35. 1

610 Aguas Calientes. A AGUSTIN Iº EMPERADOR etc. Sword and sceptre crossed beneath crown. ℞ PROCLAMADO | etc. in 6 lines, within wrth. Fon. 6748. V. fine, rare. Æ. 30. 1

611 Chiapa. Head l. ℞ CHIAPAS PROCLAMAN. etc. Fis. 372, Fon. 6925. V. fine. Æ. 20. 1

612 Durango. AGUSTIN ✶ I ✶ EMPERADOR ✶ etc. Cwnd arms. ℞ Proclama. — | do en Duran | go etc., wrth. Fis. 394, Fon. 6787. About perfect, brilliant. Æ. 34. 1

613 Another, from same dies. About perfect, partly bright. Edge diag. milling. Æ. 34. 1

614 Guadalaxara. AGUSTIN I · DIV · PROV · etc. Mil. bust r. ℞ GUADALAX. ACADEM. etc. In field, Virtute | non | sanguine. Fon. 6909. Very good, rare. Slightly elliptical. Æ. 38½ x 41. 1

615 — AGUSTIN ✶ PRIMER ✶ EMP ✶ etc. Bust as last. ℞ Guadalaxara ✶ en su Venturosa ✶ etc. 2 wolves support tree. Fon. 6910. Fine. Æ. 39½. 1

616 Guadalaxara.   Another, obv. as last.   ℞ EL CONSULADO |
NACIONAL DE | GUADALAXARA   Fis. 462, Fon. 6911.   Very
good. Æ. 39.   1

617 — Another, obv. like 588.   ℞ EN SU | AUGUSTA | PROCLA-
MACION | LA CATEDRAL DE | GUADALAXARA.   Not in Fis.
or Fon. V. rare, v. fine. Æ. 39.   1

618 Guanaxuato.   LA . N . Y . L · C . DE GUANAJUATO PROCLAMAN-
DO   Bust of Augustin and wife *r*.   ℞ Virgin in cwnd shld.
Edge of blooming roses.   Fis. 409, Fon. type 6826.   About
perfect. Æ. 36.   1

619 Oaxaca.   A · AGUSTIN Iᵒ EMPERAᴼᴿ   Bust *r*.   ℞ Lo juro | en
el ano d 1822 | etc.   Fis. 518, Fon. 6951.   Nearly perfect,
rare. Æ. 38.   1

620 — Bust *r*., by *Gordillo*.   ℞ Lo juro el 5 | de Diciembre | etc.
Fis. 519, Fon. 6952.   Very good. Æ. 27.   1

621 Queretaro.   Bust of Augustin and wife conjoined *r*., hds bare.
℞ QUERETARO FIEL Y AGRADECIDA.   Arms.   Not in Fis. or
Fon.   Fine, very rare. Æ. 38.   1

622 TOLUCA. | EN LA FELIZ | etc. in 8 lines, weak in centre. ℞
Same as 584.   Fis. 363, Fon. 6743. · Edge, diagonal milling.
V. fine, brilliant. Æ. 34.   1

623 — Another, from same dies, no weak parts.   Edge, circle and
oblong alternate.   Fis. 364.   Fine. Æ. 34.   1

624 Vera Cruz.   LA CIUDAD DE VERACRUZ Eagle.   ℞ Proclama |
por Emperador | etc. in 6 lines.   Not in Fis. or Fon.   Very
fine, very rare. Æ. 27.   1

625 — AUGUST · MEX · I · IMPERATOR etc.   Bust with order chain.
℞ NON ✳ VERACRUZ ✳ etc.   Arms.   Not in Fis. or Fon.   V.
fine. Æ. 41.   1

The rev. of this medal is from the same die as used for a Proclamation piece of
Chas. IV, 1789, with over date badly executed.

626 Zacatecas.   Eagle in cwnd shld on sword and sceptre crossed.
℞ PROCLAMADO | EN LA M. N. YL. ZACATˢ | etc. in 6 lines.
Fon. 7105.   Very fine. Æ. 32.   1

627 — Another from same dies.   Fis. 628.   Fine. Æ. 31.   1

628 Guatemala (Fis. 17, Fon. 7207), Leon de Nicaragua (not in
Fis. or Fon.), and Quezaltenago (Fis. 74, Fon. 7292), holed,
all with head *l*.   Proclamation pieces.   Good to very fine.
Æ. 20.   3

1823.

629 Bust of Aug. and wife conjoined *r.*, heads laur. ℞ AL LIBER-
TADOR A LA PATRIA etc. In 5 lines on altar, on which rest
cwn, sword and sceptre. Fis. 198, Fon. 6554. V. fine. Æ. 44.   1

630 AGUSTIN PRIMERO etc. Mil. bust *r.* ℞ En su solemne pro-
clamacion etc. Eagle on cactus; lettered edge. Fis. 201,
Fon. 6557. Fine ; a few nicks, one deep, before forehead.
Æ. 41.   1

631 A specimen of each of the 2 preceding pieces in copper, both
about perfect.   2

632 Obv. same as 600. ℞ PROTO MEDICATUS | etc. in 6 lines.
Fis. 196, Fon. 6553. Nearly perfect. Æ. 39.   1

633 AGUSTIN | PRIMER EMP | etc. in 5 lines. ℞ Eagle on flag in-
scribed La Patria etc. Edge lettered. Fis. 200, Fon. 6556.
Nearly perfect. Æ. 34.   1

634 **Provisional Government** (1823). Military medal sim. to
605 with SEGUNDA EPOCA on rev. Fine. Æ. 49.   1

635 **Republic.** Guadalupe Victoria, President, 1824. Bust *r.*
℞ REPUBLICA MEXICANA Eagle *l.* on cactus plant, legend
around border in small letters. Fis. 206, Fon. 6583. About
perfect ; brilliant. Very rare. Æ. 42.   1

636 Another from same dies as last, in copper. About perfect.
Very rare. 42.   1

637 1841. Preclarivs | Militie | Reipublice | que dux | Anton.
Lopez | de Santa Ana | Mdcccxli ℞ Et Libertatis | et
Decoris | Patrie | Fundamenta | Posvit. Fon. 6636. About
perfect. Very rare. Æ. 47.   1

638 1843. Antonius . L. De . Santa-Anna | cui . acceptas . Refer-
unt | Patria. Libertatem | etc. in 11 lines. ℞ Wreath only.
Fis. Type 236, not in Fon. Fine, rare. Æ. 65.   1

639 1843. Another from same dies as last. Fis. 236. Fine, rare.
Æ. 65.   1

640 1843. Mil. Asylum. ASILO A LA CONSTANCIA Y — AL. VALOR
MILITAR. Front of a building with 8 pillars. ℞ SE COLOCO
LA | etc. | ANTONIO LOPEZ | DE SANTA—ANNA | etc. in 8 lines.
Fon. 6644, Fis. type 234. About perfect. Æ. 40.   1

641 1843. LIBERTAD. Liberty setd *r.* ℞ Jura de la | Constitu-
cion | Mexicana | en 1843 Fis. 235, Fon. 6645. Obv. not
perfectly centered, otherwise about perfect. Æ. 28.   1

642 1851–52. War Medal. EL | CONGRESO | MEXICANA | EN | 1852
℞ ACREDITADOS EN DEFENSA DE LA FRONTERA DEL NORTE
Within wreath, AL | VALOR | Y | LEALTAD. With loop. Fis.
type 247. Brilliant; about perfect. Very rare. Æ. 25.   1

643 1855. Locomotive *r.* ℞ Primer | Camino de Fierro | de la
Capital etc. in 12 lines. Fis. 250. Fine. Æ. 46.   1

644 1880. A ULISES S. GRANT | LA ESCUELA | DE | BELLAS ARTES |
DE MEXICO | 1880 ℞ An elaborate and finely executed
Aztec Calendar shield, covering entire surface. Fis. 309.
Perfect, very rare. Æ. 41.   1

645 CALENDARIO AZTEC—MEXICO By *Ocampo.* ℞ Design like preceding. V. fine. Æ. 26.   1

646 A la Aplicacion Premio de Honor · Angel setd on cloud. ℞
La | Autoridad | de | Mexico. Wreath. V. fine. Æ. 37.   1

647 Oaxaca. 1809. FERDINAND VII · REDEAS DIUQUE etc. Bust *l.*
Ex., Prorege Arch | Lizana ℞ SANCTÆ ✠ ANTEQUERENSE
COLLEG · etc. Minerva setd *l.* rests on pedestal, holds chained
crown. Fis. 135, Fon. 6482. Æ gilt, oval. 52 x 62. Plate.   1

648 — 1814. ✳ FERDINANDO ✳ VII ✳ etc. Head *r.* ℞ ANT ✳
EPP ✳ ANTEQUER ✳ etc. Spain and Indian sup. arms on
two globes. Fis. 159, Fon. 6509. Nearly perfect. Æ.
42.   1

649 — 1814. Another, from same dies as last. Nearly perfect.
Æ gilt. 42.   1

650 Orizaba. COLEGIO DE ESTUDIOS PREPARATORIOS etc. EN ORIZA-
BA Eagle on globe holds open book. ℞ GOBIERNO DEL ES-
TADO etc. DE VERACRUZ LLAVE Lamp on closed book, hand
above dropping oil from bottle. Fis. 598. Oval, 31 x 42,
with loop. Fine. Æ.   1

651 Puebla. 1833. War Medal. EL GOBIERNO DE LA UNION A
LOS HEROICOS DEFENSORES DE PUEBLA EN 1833 ✳ ℞ LA
FEDERACION TRIUNFANT | etc. in 4 lines. Ex. S. B. G. A.
Type Fis. 533. Very fine, probably loop removed. Very
rare. Oval, 36 x 46. Æ.   1

652 — Another of same design as last, with date in field, below, the
cactus plant, with large die proj. loop. Fine, rare. Brass.
Oval, 30 x 33.   1

653 Quezaltenango. ESTELLA DE OCCIDENT N°. 15 OR.˙. C.˙. A.˙. — QUEZALTENANGO. Star, within which v.˙. L.˙. | 5634 ℞ Plain. About perfect, very rare Masonic. Æ. 34. 1

654 San Luis Potosi. 1828. EL ESTADO LIB. | etc. in 6 lines. ℞ Mexico Libre. Indian Princess setd. Fis. 546, Fon. 6967. V. fine. Æ. 29. 1

655 Silao. 1821. Religion Independencia Union. A. 821 Bust of Ferd. VII r. ℞ SILAO | CONS AGRA ESTA MEMORIA | etc. in 7 lines, wrth. Fis. 440. Fine, rare. Brass. 31. 1

656 Vera Cruz. Action of Monte de las Cruces. 1810. FER-NANDO · VII · REY etc. Bust r. in small oval above battle scene. ℞ AL | EXMO . SOR . VENEGAS | etc. VERA CRUZ in 11 lines. Fon. 7048, Fis. type 601. Nearly perfect, rare. Æ. 54. 1

657 — 1825. War Medal. A LA HEROICA DEFENSA DEL CASTILLO DE SAN JUAN DE ULUA View of castle, date below. ℞ POR | FERNANDO | 7° Nearly fine, extremely rare. Æ. 36½. 1

658 Zacatecas. 1829. War Medal. EL ESTADO DE ZACATECAS AL VENCEDOR DE TAMPICO Forts on hills resting on military trophy. ℞ Mexican eagle within wrth, backed by flags, etc. Very fine and rare. Æ. Oval, 38 x 50, die proj. loop. 1

In July, 1829, Brig.-Gen. Barradas, with 4,000 Spanish troops disembarked at Cabo Rojo, near Tampico, but was compelled to capitulate on September 11.

658a 1865. TORNARE A NUEVA etc. Eagle on crossed oak branches, holds serpent in his talons, radiated civic crown above. ℞ A | CAMILLO CAVOUR | E | SALVATORE VILLAMARIA | etc. ITALIANI NEL MESSICO in 9 lines. By Thermignon. *Trans.* The Italians of Mexico to Camillo Cavour and Salvatore Villamaria, who at the Congress of Paris, in the name of Italy, raised their voices. Very fine and rare. Æ. 55. 1

THE SECOND EMPIRE.

COINS AND MEDALS OF MAXIMILIAN AND OTHER MEDALS OF HIS TIME.

WAR MEDALS.

659 **French Intervention.** Nap. III, head *l.* By *Barre.* ℞ Expedition du Mexique — 1862 . 1863. In field, Cumbres | Cerro-Barrego | San-Lorenzo | Puebla | Mexico. Loop, ring and ribbon. Very fine, brilliant. Æ. 31. 1

660 Another of similar design with larger head, By *E. Falot.* Ribbon. Perfect. Rare. Æ. 31.   1

661 Another with slightly differing head. Signed *E.F.* Ribbon. Perfect. Rare. Æ. 31.   1

662 A miniature of the preceding medal. Ribbon. Perfect. Æ. 18.   1

663 A design sim. to 659, signed *Sacristain F.* Ribbon. Nearly perfect. Rarer than either of the preceding. Æ. 31.   1

-664 Another *without* initials or name of engraver. Ribbon. Nearly perfect. Rare. Æ. 31.   1

665 A miniature of the preceding, with ribbon. About perfect. Æ. 15.   1

666 Another sim. and the smallest of the series. V. fine. Æ. 12½.   1

667 **Maximilian.** MAXIMILIANO EMPERADOR. Head *l.* By *C. T.* ℞ AL | MERITO | MILITAR within wreath. Loop, ring and ribbon. About perfect. Æ. 34.   1

668 Another similar with head *r.* By *E. Falot.* Loop, ring and ribbon. About perfect. Æ. 33.   1

669 Another from same dies as last. Æ, bronzed. Perfect. 33.   1

670 Another sim. to 668, signed *Navalon. G.* on rev. Loop and ring. V. fine. Æ. 32.   1

671 Another from same dies as last; a bronzed proof, shows slight handling. 32.   1

672 Another obv. from same die as 670. ℞ AL | MERITO | CIVIL within wreath, signed *Navalon. G.* on rev. Loop only. V. fine. Æ. 33.   1

673 Another from same dies as last. Loop and ring. Fine. Æ. 33. Also a miniature of the same, signed *S. N. G.* on rev., without loop. Perfect. Æ. 14½.   2

674 Head *l.* A very close copy of 667, signed on obv. *Stern. F.* Accent mark above E in MERITO. Loop, ring and ribbon. About perfect. Æ. 34.   1

675 Another from same dies as last. Loop and ring. Fine. Æ. 34.   1

676 Head *r.*, closely resembling 671. Unsigned. Large letters in legend. ℞ From same die as 674. Loop and ring. Nearly perfect, rare. Æ gilt. 34.   1

677 Miniature Military Medal. Head *r.* General type of preceding. Unsigned. Loop, ring and ribbon. Perfect. Æ. 16.   1

678 A variety of last. Loop and ring. About perfect. Æ. 15.   1

679 Others still differing, one signed *S. N. G.* on rev. Without loop. Æ. 14. Another, unsigned. Loop, ring and ribbon. Æ gilt. 16. Both about perfect. 2

680 **Defenders of the Republic.** PREMIO—AL PATRIOTISMO In field, inscription, COOPERO | A LA | DEFENSA | DE LA | REPUBLICA | etc. in 7 lines. ℞ DISTINTIVO—AL VALOR In field, COMBATIO | POR LA | INDEPENDENCIA | etc. in 6 lines. Size 21, on radiated cross. Loop. Fis. 283. Fine. Æ. 46½. 1

681 1862. Acultzingo Heights Ap. 28ᵗʰ. COMBATIO | CON HONOR | EN LAS | etc. in 9 lines. ℞ La | Republicana | Mexicana | etc. in 6 lines, signed *S. N. G.* Loop and ribbon bar. V. good, rare. Æ. Oval. 21 x 26. 1

682 Oaxaca. DEFENDIO | LA | INDEPENDENCIA | NACIONAL | OAX-ACA. ℞ VENCIENDO | AL | ENEMICO | ESTRANGERO Y AL | TRAIDOR A SU PATRIA. Against all foreigners and traitors. Size 31. Attached to a small eagle, pin or ribbon slide, broken. Good, very rare. Æ. 1

683 Puebla, May 5th, 1862. GRAL IGNACIO ZARAGOZA — VEN-CEDOR DE LOS FRANCESES Head *r.* ℞ Mayo | 5 | 1862 on radiated field. Loop. Fine. Æ. Also Æ, very good. 28. 2

684 — DEFENDIENDO A LA CIUDAD | DE | PUEBLA | etc. EL 5 DE MAYO DE 1862 in 9 lines. ℞ LA | REPUBLICA | MEXICANA | A SUS | VALIENTES | HIJOS Loop, bar and ribbon. V. fine and rare. Æ. 26. 1

685 — DERROTANDO A LOS TRAIDORES | EL 4 DE MAYO | CONTRI-BUYO | etc. EL 5 DE MAYO 1862 in 9 lines. By *Navalon.* ℞ From same die as last. Loop. V. fine. Æ. 26. 1

686 — TRIUNFO | GLORIOSAMENT | DEL EJERCITO FRANCES | etc. DE 1862 in 8 lines. ℞ From same die as 681. Probably loop removed. Fine. Æ. Oval 21 x 26. 1

687 — El Estado de Puebla | Premia | el Valor | y | la Constancia ℞ Combatio | por la | Independencia | de su Patria. Loop, ring, ribbon and bar depending. Eagle on cactus plant. Fine, very rare. Æ. 24. 1

688 — ASALTO LA LOS DE PUEBLA — 2 DE ABRIL DE 1867 etc. ℞ El Estado de Puebla | al | Valor | Militar. Fis. 538. Good. Æ. 26½. 1

⌐/ **689** Guanaxuato mint. 1864 10 Ctvs. 1865 5 and 10 do. 1866
5 do. Good to v. fine.   4

⌐‹ **690** Mexico mint. 1864 Centavo. Unc., red, rare. 21.   1

691 1864 5 Ctvs., unc., 10 do., fine. 1866 5 do., holed, 10 do., fine. 4

692 1866 50 Centavos. Very fine.   1

693 1866 Peso. Obv. die shows a very slight break from point of
nose and at back of head. V. fine. A trifle less than unc.   1

·**694** 1866 Another with MAXIMILIANO EMPERADOR in much larger
letters. A break in die below nose to R and through head
to I (after M). It is said few were struck from this die. Very
fine. Rare.   1

/. **695** 1867 Peso. Scarce date. Nearly fine.   1

696 San Luis Potosi mint (P), 1864 10 Ctvs. Fine. Zacatecas
mint, 1865 5 do. Fine. 10 do. V. good.   3

MEDALS.

⸴ **697** Heads of MAXIMILIANO Y CARLOTA EMPERADORES conjoined *l.*,
small laurel branch at either side. By *Ocampo*. ℞ Aztec
calendar. Probably at one time used as a reversible pin.
Very fine, rare. Æ. Gilt. 33.   1

698 Hd *r.* *Navalon D. Ocampo G.* ℞ AL | MERITO | CIENTIFICO |
Y | ARTISTICO. About perfect, rare. Æ. 45.   1

⸴⸴ **699** Obv. from same die as last. ℞ HONOR A LA JUVENTUD ESTU-
DIOSA. Wrth, plain field. V. fine, rare. Æ. 45.   1

700 MAX KAISER VON MEXICO. Mil. bust facing. ℞ CHARLOTTE
KAISERIN etc. Bust ¾ *l.* Nearly perfect, v. rare. W.m. 32.   1

⸴ **701** M. CARLOTA EMPERATRIZ Hd *l.* ℞ AL | MERITO | CIVIL with-
in wrth, below, *S. N. G.* Probably loop removed. V. good,
very rare. Æ. 14½.   1

702 1863 Hd *l.* ℞ Junta de los notables etc. Fis. 262. Fine.
Brass. 21.   1

703 1865 Head of Max. *l.* by *N. D — Ocampo . G* ℞ NON FECIT
TALITER etc. Our Lady of Guadalupe. Fis. 265. V. fine.
Æ. 28.   1

704 — Another, from same dies as last. Small spot at point of
whiskers, otherwise about perfect. Æ. 28.   1

705 — Head of Max. and Carlotta conjoined *l.* ℞ Type of 703,
signed *A. Spirita. G* Type Fis. 266. Fine. Æ. 32½.   1

706   1866 Another, same type as last and by same artists, but quite
differently executed. Fis. 266, Fon. 6701. V. fine. Æ. 32½.   1

707   — Another, from same die as last. V. fine. Æ. 32½.   1

708   1867. MAXIMILIAN I. + 19 JUNI 1867 Head *r.* by *A. Pittner.*
℞ Arms of Austria and Mexico depending from crown. V.
good, rare. Æ. 32½.   1

709   — Another, from same dies as last, circle of black around
border. About perfect, rare. W.m. 32½.   1

710   — Head *r.* by *A. Kleeburg.* ℞ NATUS 6. JULII 1832 — + 19.
JUNII 1867 Angel setd beside tomb. Fon. 6707. 2 slight
dents on obv., 1 on rev., otherwise nearly perfect, very rare.
W.m. 41.   1

711   — Head *r.* signed *A. K.* ℞ Imp. arms supported. Legends
sim. to last. Fis. 271, Fon. 6708. Brass, perfect ; die proj.
loop ; also W.m., without loop. V. good. 22½.   2

712   — Obv. from same die as 697. ℞ 12 | de Junio | de 1864 |
19 | de Junio | de 1867 within wrth. Fis. 272. Nearly per-
fect. Very rare. Æ. 31.   1

713   — AL C? PRESIDENTE | BENITO JUAREZ | EN SU VUELTA | A S.?
LUIS POTOSI | FEBRERO DE | 1867. ℞ The Mexican eagle,
shadowed by the rays from liberty cap, above a military
trophy. Commemorates the arrival of Juarez as President at
San Luis Potosi. Fine and extremely rare. By *Flolet.* Æ.
47.   1

MEXICAN PATTERNS FOR COINS.

714   1822 Augustin. Head *r.* ℞ Eagle on cactus, field plain.
Milled borders. 8 Rls. Different from any coined, as are
also the three following lots. Silver shells, obv. and rev.
separate. Very fine, extremely rare.   1

715   1823 Repub. 8. R. M̃. 1823. J. M. etc. Lib. cap on rays. LIB-
ERTAD on cap above band or roll. ℞ Hook-necked eagle.
Beaded borders. V. fine, extremely rare. Æ.   1

716   1825 A very dif. Liberty cap banded with ribbon, having bow
r. Sparse rays. M̃. 8 R.S J. M. etc. deployed around border.
Very fine, extremely rare. Æ.   1

717   1827 8 R : 1827 : W : W : etc. Liberty cap on small plain field,
within circular radiation. ℞ Usual type. Borders with point s
of nopal leaves. An exceedingly rare and beautiful design.
By *Wm. Wyon.* In proof condition. Æ.   1

−718 1832–33 ½, 2, 4, and 8 Escudos. Hand holds Lib. cap on staff before open book. Durango mint. Diagonal milling on edges. Very fine. A little scratched. Rare. Brass. 4

719 1831–33 ½, 1, 2 and 8 Rls. Durango mint. Usual type even to finished edges. Very fine. Portion of two R. very weak. Very rare. White metal. 4

720 1836 Cuartilla. Lib. cap on plain field encircled by small clouds from which extend rays. Fis. 227, Fon. 6628. Very fine. Æ. 27. 1

721 1838 Liberty head r. Date bet. large 8 ptd. stars. ℞ UNA | CUARTILLA | Cᴬ within a milled circle; border of oak leaves and acorns. Fon. 6765. Very fine, about unc. Very rare. Brass. 28. 1

722 1838 Obv. as last. ℞ ESTADO DE CHIHUAHUA. Indian stdg. with bow and arrow. Fon. 6750. Fine, very rare. Brass. 29. 1

723 1838 Same. ℞ UNA | CUARTILLA | D⁰ above oak branches, crossed. Fon. 6808. Very fine, very rare. Brass. 28½. 1

724 1838 Same. ℞ 1 | CUARTILLA | Gᴬ within cartouche. Fon. 6914. V. fine and rare. Brass. 28. 1

725 1838 Same. ℞ UNA | CUARTILLA | G⁰ within wrth of oak and olive branches. Fon. 6848. V. fine and rare. Brass. 28½. 1

726 1838 Same. ℞ UNA | CUARTILLA | M⁰. Leaf-points around border. Fon. 6633. V. fine, v. rare. Brass. 28½. 1

727 1838 A dif. and smaller head. ℞ UNA | CUARTILLA | Ṁ. Wrth of oak and olive branches. Not in Fon. Fine, very rare. Brass. 28½. 1

728 1838 Same as 721. ℞ CUARTILLA—S. L. P. A large 1 in field within a beaded circle. Not in Fon. V. fine, v. rare. Brass. 28. 1

729 1838 Same. ℞ UNA | CUARTILLA | Zˢ Wreath of oak and olive branches. Not in Fon. V. fine, v. rare. Brass. 30. 1

730 1844 8 Rls. Usual type. By *M. M.* With *milled* edge. Brzd proof, from the Fischer collection. 1

731 1865 8 Escudo (or Doubloon), Hermosillo mint. Herring-bone edge; borders not well struck, otherwise fine. In silver. 39. 1

— 732 Impression of reverse (on eagle side) of 8 Rls. Fine. Æ. 39. 1865 UNIVERSAL REMEDY above a finely executed Mexican eagle. Perfect. W.m. 47. 2

'⌐733 Equestrian ornaments, 1828, '31, etc., imitating devices of Mexican coins. Brass. V. fine. 27, 38 (2).   3

734 Eu!. Kurtz | Mécanicien | a Paris ℟ Monnaie Mexicaine. Eagle on cactus. Æ. 31. Brass. 37. Also Jeton, "La Libertad." 22. Fine.   3

735 Uruachic. 1873 N. y. E. Rascon Hermanos. 25, 50 and 100 Ctvs. ℟ Eagle, etc. Fon. 6745-47. Perfect. Brass. 28, 31, 35.   3

736 **Catholic Church Medals.** *Silver.* All with loop excepting St. Gerda. Ameca, 1827. Fine. Oval. 31 x 33. Mexico, 1788, image of Los Remedios. Very good. Oval. 28 x 34.   2

737 Mexico, 1795 (the 9 reversed). Our Lady Guadalupe. Very fine. 35. 1797, Los Remedios. Fis. 108. Fine. Oval, 27 x 32.   2

738 1797 Our Lady Guadalupe. Fine. Oval, 28 x 35; also one of same date and design, 19 x 22. Very fine.   2

739 1800 St. Teresa. Good. Oval, 28 x 32. 1830, S. S. Jose. Refugio de Agonizartes. Very fine. 33.   2

740 John Nepomuc. ℟ Ins. in 11 lines. Oval, 26 x 32. Tepaczingo. ℟ san jorge martir St. George killing dragon. 30; also the Trinity setd. 32. All fine.   3

741 **Others.** Mexico, 1780. Our Lady Guadalupe on 4 cornered 35 x 43. Æ. 1802. Fon. 6453 (W.m.) 1805 (2 var.) Brass. Tlalnepantla. Crucifixion. Brass. Oval, 28 x 35. Tepaczingo, Madre Dolorosa etc. Æ. 30. Fine to perfect.   6

VARIOUS.

742 Haiti. henry le grand president etc. 1811. Mil. bust *r.* ℟ la religion etc. Sun rising from sea horizon. Not in Fon. Very good. Loop removed. Extremely rare. Æ. Gilt. 39.   1

743 Porto Rico. Isabel II. Bust *l.* Small medal of the Royal Academy. Fine. Æ. 21.   1

744 Pichincha (1822). el peru — en pichincha. Shield inscribed, a | los liber | tadores | de quito. ℟ la patria agradecida. Sun in rays. War Medal. Fon. 8333. Holed near edge for ring or ribbon. Very fine and rare. Æ. 25 x 29.   1

745 Buenos Ayres. Chas. IV, 1806. LA * LEALTAD * DE * BUE-
NOS-AIRES * A * SU * REI * CARLOS IIII * * * Bust *r.*
℞ QUISO SER VENCEDOR . YA ESTA VENCIDO — DIA XII DE —
AGOSTO DE M'DCCC'VI Lion holds flag of Spain setd. on staff
of English flag which lies upon the ground. Fon. 10060.
An extremely rare, valuable and interesting medal, struck to
commemorate the Spaniards' recapture of the city from the
British. Very fine. ℞. 50.   1

746 — VIVA LA EXCELENTISIMA JUNTA Ship, anchor and bird in
oval. ℞ DE LA CAPITAL DE BUENOS AIRES Lion on trophy,
holds label ins. ANO DE 1811. V. fine. Planchet is com-
posed of three parts. The obv. and rev. are silver, while the
centre is lead. 30.   1

747 Bruges ("in the 13th and 14th centuries, almost the commer-
cial metropolis of the world "). Chas. II of Spain. Tournay.
Phil. IV. Jetons, both with bust. Good. Æ. 28, 33.   2

748 Spain. Chas. VI, 1716. Satirical. V. fine. Æ. 25. Also
Proclamation Jetons, Ferd. VII, 1812, for Segovia. 2 var.
V. fair. Æ. 26. And a medal with his portrait. Good,
holed. W.m. 40.   4

749 Alcala la Real. Charles III, 1759. Holed, poor. ℞. 21.
Gerunda, 1789. V. fine. ℞. 17. Ferd. VII, Seville, 1823.
V. good. ℞. 19.   3

750 Chas. III (VI of Germany), 1705. Bust *r.* ℞ EXPECTATO
VINDICI etc. The King receiving the Spanish crown at
Madrid, Oct. 14th, 1705. Inscribed edge. Fine. ℞. 32.   1

751 BERGA—27 DE MARZO DE 1873 Head of Don Carlos *r.* ℞
DIOS PATRIA Y REY Cwned arms. Loop and ring. About
perfect. Æ. 34.   1

752 Valladolid, 1855. Opening of R. R. Fine, unc. 35. Flaming
shell, cannon crossed below; behind, circular band ins.
STANDARD. ℞ Plain. Fine, unc. 39.   2

753 Bust *l.* By *A. Sch·*(arf). ℞ Societas | Nvmismatica | Vin-
dobonensis (Vienna) etc. 1880. In 8 lines. Nearly perfect.
Æ. 35.   1

754 Phil. V, 1711. Bust *r.* By *J. C. R.*(oettier) ℞ REGNI · SUO ·
VICTORI · AC TRIUMPHANTI ·—AN 1711 · S. P. Q. P. (Pal-
ermo ?) on cartouch, above which the Sicilian eagle. Fine,
rare. Æ. 42.   1

755 Adelphi Cotton Works, Beehive, 1838, Halfpennies. Philippine Islands. Chas. IV, 1807; Ferd. VII, 1829. Quartos. Good ; 3 are rare.   4

756 Ancient Rome, B. C. 338–268. Bifrons head of Janus. ℞ Prow of ship, above, 1   A fine and very desirable specimen of the Roman As. Weight, 8½ oz.   1

SPANISH-AMERICAN PROCLAMATION COINS AND MEDALS.

Silver, unless otherwise stated. Many letters in the legend, etc., in monograms and Ns reversed which cannot be represented in type.

FLORIDA.

CHARLES III. Proclaimed 11 September, 1759.

757 1760 CARLOS . (the AR is in monogram) III . D. G. HISPAN . REX Bust *r*. ℞ JVAN . ESTEVAN . DE PENA . FLORIDA — 1760 A large blooming rose on stem with leaves. Holed near edge, otherwise good. A rude original cast. Not in Herrera. Exceptionally rare. 31. B. 454.   1

758 1760 Another of same design, but better perfected and struck from dies. From the Fonrobert collection, lot 1510, where it brought 51 Marks. Fine.   31.   1

WEST INDIES.

LOUIS I. Proclaimed 17 January, 1724.

759 **Havana.** LVIS PR R D ESPA Bust *r*. ℞ HABANA — AQENDO Two keys in field. Orig. cast. Not in H. Holed above head, otherwise good. Extremely rare. 20. Plate.   1

FERDINAND VI. Proclaimed 10 August, 1746.

760 **Guanabacoa.** 1747. Bust *r*. with usual titles. ℞ SANTIAGO DE TORES . GVANA? In field two castles. H. 41, B. 344. Orig. cast. Very good. Very rare. 29.   1

761 **Havana.** 1747. Obv. very sim to last. ℞ GONZALO. REZIO DE OQVENDO HABº 1747. In field two keys. H. 46. B. 349. Orig. cast. Has been broken through centre, and well mended, otherwise good. 29.   1

762 **Santiago de Cuba.** 1747 FERD. VI . HISP ET INDIARVN . REX + on raised border. Bust *r*. ℞ IOAN . DE CAXIGAL P . CVB . ERCLAMAT + on raised border. Mtd horseman *l*., date below. H. 60, B. 364. Orig. cast. V. good, rare. 26½.   1

CHARLES III.   Proclaimed 11 September, 1759.

763   **Havana.** 1760 CARLOS · III · D · G · HISPAN · REX   A very
close copy of 757.   ℞ GONZALO · REZIO · DE OQVENDO · HA-
BANA ·   Three castles and key, placed in cross form. H. 66,
B. 464, Fon. 7738.   Orig. cast; holed near edge. V. good,
extremely rare. 33.   1

764   **Santa Maria del Rosario.** 1760 CAROLUS . III . D . G . HIS-
PAN . REX . in large letters.   ℞ JhP. RVIZ. S. M. R. ✢ ✢ ✢
Bird on top of tree, roots exposed ; below, 1760. Not in H.
Orig. cast.   M. F. lightly cut in rev. field, otherwise fine.
29½.   Plate.   1

CHARLES IV.   Proclaimed 17 January, 1789.

765   **Guanabacoa.** 1789 CAROLUS · IV · DEI · GRATIA ·   Bust *r.*
MICAEL NUNES GUANAVACOA   Two castles on rocky founda-
tion. A slight var. of H. 139.   Orig. cast.   Good ; plugged
above head ; extremely rare. 36.   1

766   1789 Another. CAROLUS IV · DI GTA   Bust *r.* ℞ MIGUEL
NUNES GUANABACOA   Two castles in mid-air, rocks below,
water above. H. 140. Orig. cast. Very good, extremely
rare. 30.   1

767   **Havana.** 1789 Bust *r.*, with titles and date. ℞ MIGUEL ·
CIRIACO · ARANCO · HABANA   Three castles above crossed
keys. H. 150. Orig. cast. Good, holed above head, rare.
H. values at 50 Pesetas. 28½.   1

768   1789 Another sim. but better work. CAROLUS IV · etc., with
HANBA in mon. Three castles with one key below. H. 151.
Orig. cast. Fine, holed above head, very rare. 21½.   1

769   **Matanzas.** 1789 Obv. from same mould as last. ℞ JUAN .
DEDIOS . MOREJON . M. T. S.   In field, a castle with flag. H.
159. Orig. cast. Very good, holed, rare. 21½.   1

770   **San Domingo.** 1789 CAROLO IV. HISP. ET IND. R. F. O. and
date (in legend). Bust *r.*, with an ill-proportioned nose.
HISPANIOLA OFFE^RT ℞ PRIM . POSTCASTELL. Lions support
key, crown above. Not in H. Orig. cast. Fine and extremely rare. 31.   Plate.   1

771   **Trinidad de Cuba.** 1789 CAROLUS · IIII ✳ ✳ DEI GRATIA ·
Bust *r.* ℞ MANUEL · DE SOTO LONGO · TRINIDAD Arms in
shld, supported. A slight var. of H. 226. Orig. cast. Fine,
rare. 26.   1

772 **Villa Clara.** 1790 CAROLUS · IV · · H. ET I. R. P. Bust *r.* ;
below, *Ant° Gallo* ℞ Vase with grapes, etc., above UBER-
TAS . below V–C. 1790. Unpublished. Coarse work, from
dies. Fine. 29.   1

ISABELLA II. Proclaimed 2 October, 1833.

773 **Bejucal.** 1834 Isabel II. Cwnd arms of the city. ℞ Ac-
clamatio | Avgvsta | xxx. Mart · | Mdcccxxxiv | s. FPE. YSGO.
V. good, holed. 21. H. 40.   1

774 **Guanabacoa.** 1834 Spanish arms. ℞ Antonio Santalla de
Elias. City arms, now clearly developed into water, castles,
and a rocky point, each separately arranged in shield. Edge
milled. Fine. H. 41, Fon. 7737 ; Cat. 4, 185. 26.   1

775 1834 Another from same dies. Edge, "Dios conserve la
Reina." V. fine. 26.   1

776 **Guines.** 1834 Elizabeth II, etc. City arms in cwnd shield.
℞ Sim. to 773, last line GUINES. H. 44. V. fine, brilliant,
rare. 21.   1

777 **Havana.** 1834 City arms cwnd. ℞ Acclamatio | Avgvsta |
VIII · Feb · | Mdcccxxxiv | Habana. H. 45. F. 7739. Very
fine. 31.   1

778 1834 Another of same design. H. 46, F. 7740 ; Cat. 4, 186.
V. fine. 21.   1

779 **Jaruco.** 1834 Sim. to to 777. City arms. ℞ Acclamatio |
Avgvsta | xxx. Mart. | Mdcccxxxiv | Jaruco. Rev. has broad
milled border. H. 47. Very fine, rare. 29.   1

780 **Matanzas.** 1834 Type as last ; different arms and VIII ·
FEB · etc. MATANZAS. H. 48, F. 7743 ; Cat. 4, 195. Fine,
holed. 29.   1

781 **Porto Rico.** 1834 ISAB. II | REIᴬ DE ESPᴬ E | INDᴺ PROCLᴰᴬ
| EN PTO. RICO | ANO DE | 1834 ℞ ESMNIML POR SU etc. |
(All n's reversed) Paschal lamb. A bold original cast. Fine,
extremely rare. H. 49, who values it at 50 Pesetas. 38.   1

782 **San Antonio Abad.** 1834 Type same as 777, with xxx.
MART. and V. S. ANT. AB H. 51, F. 7748. Fine, holed, rare.
21.   1

783 **Santa Maria del Rosario.** 1834 Spanish arms, type of
774. ℞ JUAN NEPOMUCENO MONTERO etc. H. 53, F. 7745 ;
Cat. 4, 199. V. fine. 26.   1

784   **Santiago de las Vegas.** 1834 Obv. from same die as 774.
℞ FELIX QUINTERO—etc. Arms sep. 4º DE—MAYO. H. 55 ;
Cat. 4, 201. Nearly perfect, brilliant. 26.   1

785   **Trinidad.** 1834 ISABEL ˙ II ˙ REINA ˙ DE ˙ ESPANA ˙ E ˙ INDIAS ˙
Bust r. ℞ ALEJO ˙ ISNAGA ˙ ALFEREZ ˙ Rᵗ TRINIDAD ˙ Spanish arms. H. 59, F. 7747. Orig. cast. V. good, holed, extremely rare. 32.   1

786   1834 Another, very sim. to preceding, with date on *rev.* instead
of obv. AD in Trinidad in mon. H. 60. Orig. cast. Fine
and extremely rare. 32.   1

787   **Villa Clara.** 1834 PᵀE.LAFˢ RL. D. J. RODRIGVE Bust r. ℞
ESPRO ˙ | CLAMA= | DA ISABEL | II VILLA CLA | RA H. 61. A
very crude orig. cast. Fine, holed, rare. 24.   1

AMADEUS. Proclaimed 3 *December,* 1870.

788   **Havana.** AMADEO PRIMERO Bust r. ℞ Arms of Castile
and Leon and those of Havana in separate shields, side by
side, between pillars, civic crown above. Loop and ring.
H. 2. V. fine. 32.   1

ALFONSO XII.

789   **Havana.** 1875 Bust facing, head turned slightly r. within
branches, crossed. ℞ CIUDAD DE LA HABANA etc. in 12
lines. H. 1. Fine. Æ. 33.   1

790   A sim. bust, within branches, but differently executed, with
blank reverse. Not in H. Very fine. Æ. 33.   1

MEXICO.

PHILIP V.

791   **Mexico.** 1701 Bust r., date in legend. ℞ IMPERATOR. + IN-
DIARVM. Castle supported by lions, cactus plant in its tower,
on which eagle r., MEX — ICO H. 6, B. 89. An original
artistic cast in the finest preservation. Rare. 30.   1

LOUIS I.

792   **Mexico.** 1724 LUDOUICUS . I . etc. Bust r. ℞ Type of preceding, with eagle's head l. H. 19, B. 150, F. 6279 (from
which this identical piece came). Original cast. Fine,
holed. 38½.   1

793 **San Felipe.** 1724 Obv. from same pattern as 792. ℞ IM-
PERATOR . INDIARUM Cwnd arms of Spain, below, S. PHE.
EL REAL H. 25, B. 153. From the Fischer Catalogue, No.
438. Fine original cast, exceptionally rare. 36½.   1

794 **Vera Cruz.** 1724 LVDOV. I. D. G. HISPANIAR. R Bust *r.*
℞ VERACRUCIS . PROCLAMATIO . 1724 Castle in sea. H. 22,
B. 155. A fine orig. cast and very rare. 31.   1

CHARLES III.

795 **Cordova.** 1760 CAROL . III . ANTQ . ET NOV . HISPA . REX
Bust *r.* (Probably by *Madero.*) ℞ INSIGN FIDELIT etc.
VILLÆ DE CORDU. Cwnd arms of Spain. H. 55, B. 453.
Very fine, some orig. color. Æ. 33.   1

796 **Guadalaxara.** 1760 CAROLVS III. VET. REX. etc. A similar
bust to last, and easily judged to be by the same artist. ℞
EPIS. ET. CAP. S. CATHED. GVADALAX. etc. Arms of cardinal
and bishop. Ex., *A. B. Madero | F.* H. 58, B. 456. Very
fine, brilliant, partly bright. Very rare. Æ. 39.   1

797 **Mexico.** 1760 CAROL. III. D. G. HISPAN. REX MEXIC. PROCL.
Bust *r.*, sim. to 796. ℞ INSIGN FIDELIT etc. Arms of the
city. Ex., *A. B. Madero | F.* H. 75, B. 473. From Fon.
sale, lot 6348. V. fine, rare. Æ. 43.   1

798 1760 Another. CAROL. III ANTIQ. ET NOV. HISPᴬᴺ REX MEXIC
PROCLAM Bust *r.* By *A. B. Madero.* ℞ Insign. etc. Type
as last, edge inscribed. H. 76, B. 474. Very fine and very
rare. 38½.   1

799 1760 Another. CAROL ' III VET ' NOVAE etc. Head *r.* By
F. Casanova. ℞ EMAN. ARCHIEP. MEX etc. Arms of the
archbishop. Ex., MDCCLX H. 81, B. 479, Fis. 66, Fon. type
6347. Nearly fine. Æ. 40.   1

800 **Oaxaca.** 1760 CAROLI * III * CVIVS. EST. etc. Bust *r.*, below, OAXACA ℞ HISP. ET. IND. etc. PROCLA * Lion *r.* in
cwnd shld; below, GRANDELLANA (probably the engraver).
Not in Herrera. Rather crude work; plugged above head,
otherwise very fair. Extremely rare. 35. Plate.   1

801 **Uncertain.** 1780 CAROL III ' DEI GPTA Bust *r.* ℞ HIS'PA
ET DRM ' ? X ' CPL ' (or V.) A three-legged pot suspended
from cwn bet. pillars. The crudest design and execution;
some of the letters given are conjectural. Fine. Lead. 35.
Plate.   1

See A. J. N., Oct. 1897, for possible explanation.

CHARLES IV.

802 **Campeche.** 1790 Proclamado * en * Campeche * por * Jvan * Pedro * Ytvralde *   Cwnd arms of the city.   ℞ MAGNE * ET * AUGUST | etc. in 5 lines.   H. 122, Fis. 609, Fon. 7052.   V. fine, brilliant. 39.   1

803 1790 Others of same design.   H. 123, 124.   Nearly perfect. 28, 21.   2

804 1790 Others from dies of preceding, in copper, with correct edges.   H. 122, 123, 124.   Fine 1, unc. 2.   3

805 **Chiapa.** 1789 CAROL · IV · etc.   Bust *r.*   Acclamatio Avgvsta.   In field, Ciudad | Real de | Chiapa · a | * 1789 *   H. 127.   Good, holed, rare. 20.   1

806 **Chihuahua.** 1790 CAROL · IV · D · VOCAT · INDIAR · IMPERA · P. A. TRIVMPH   Bust *r.*   ℞ JVDEX ECCLES & CLERVS CHI- HVHV ·   In field, a crown (?) or beretta.   Not in H.   Orig. cast.   Very good, uncommonly rare. 38.   Plate.   1

807 1790 CAROLUS † IV † VOCAT † etc.   Bust *r.*   ℞ V. Parochus † Judex † etc.   A beretta within a halo resting on pedestal. H. 128, Fon. 6723.   Fine, a few nicks on obv.   Æ gilt. 47.   1

808 **Durango.** 1790 CAROL * IV * etc. DURANG * PROCLAM * Bust *r.*   ℞ IMPERATOR * INDIARUM * etc.   Two wolves passing *l.*, one before tree, the other behind, in shld, cwnd. H. 132.   Very fine, very rare. 38.   1

809 1790 Another, from same dies as preceding.   Fine.   Æ. 28.   1

810 **Guadalaxara.** 1789 Bust *r.*, with titles, and FAUSTE * PRO- CLAM * M * DCCLXXXIX   ℞ Arms of city and Papal arms, beneath cardinal's hat.   H. 137, Fis. type 461, Fon. 6905 (from which last sale this specimen came).   Fine, rare. 39.   1

811 **Guanaxuato.** 1790 CARLO * III * etc. DE LAS * YNDS Bust *r.*   ℞ FUE * PROCAMADO (*sic*) * POR * LA * NOBLE * CIUDAD DE GUANAXUATO etc.   Saint in oval, cwnd shield. H. 142 (50 Pesetas), Type Fis. 406.   V. good. 47.   1

812 1790 A CARLOS * IIII * Y * LUISA * etc.   Bust of King and Queen conjoined.   ℞ PROCLAMO * EN * GUANAXUATO * etc. Cwnd arms.   H. 143 (60 Pesetas), Fis. 405, Type Fon. 6823.   Fine. 46.   1

813 1790 CARLOS † IIII † REY † etc., in large letters. Bust *r*. ℞ ACLAMADO * EN * LA * C * DE * GUANAJUATO etc. Interior view of silver mine. H. 144 (45 Pesetas), Fis. 407, Fon. 6824. Fine, some light nicks. 47.   1

814 1790 Another from same dies as last. Somewhat nicked, still about good. Æ. 46.   1

815 1790 A variety of the preceding. Hair curls down back; Golden Fleece invisible. Rev. also differs in almost every detail. Not in H. Fine, a few light scratches; both dies cracked. Æ gilt. 47.   1

816 ° Mexico. 1789 * A * CARLOS * etc. LAS * INDIAS * Bust *r*., draped with ribbon, suspending decoration. ℞ * EN * SU * EXALTACION * etc. Cwnd arms of the city on eagle resting on bow. H. 160, Fis. 92, Type Fon. 6409. V. fine. 45.   1

817 1789 Another, from same dies as last. Fine. Æ. 47.   1

818 1789 Cwnd Spanish arms bet. pillars. ℞ PROCLAMA- | DO * EN * MEXI- | CO * ANO * DE. | 1789. | * 8 R * H. 161, Type Fis. 97, Fon. 6410. Fine. 40.   1

819 1789 Another, from same dies as last. Edge plain; *restrike*. About perfect. 40.   1

820 1789 Same type as 818. For 4 Reals. H. 162, Fis. 96, Fon. 6411. V. fine. 35.   1

821 1789 Others for 2, 1 (both uncirculated) and ½ Real, (good, holed). H. 163, 164, 165.   3

822 1789 Others, from same dies, for 4, 2 (2 varieties) and 1 Real. All original, with correct edges. Unc.; 1 a proof. Æ.   4

823 1789 * CAROLO * IV * HISP * etc. MEX * PROCL * AN * Bust *r*. ℞ * LVDOV * REG * etc. Bust of the Queen *l*. H. 166, Types Fis. 90, Fon. 6405. Very fine. 42.   1

824 1789 Another, from same dies as last. Fine. Æ. 42.   1

825 1789 A variety of last, date in legend, without Order of Golden Fleece. Rev. also differs in most details. H. 167, Fis. 89, Fon. 6404. About perfect. Æ. 42.   1

826 1789 Bust *r*., sim. to 810. Long legend, unabbreviated, beginning and ending beneath bust. ℞ * A * su * proclamacion * etc. Mercury suptg cwnd arms of the Consulate, ship *r*. H. 168, Fis. 86. Type F. 6406. Nick before forehead, otherwise v. fine. Æ. 42.   1

827   1789 CAROLO * IV * etc. FELICITER * INAUGURATO * Bust
r., with elaborate order chain. ℞ REG. FOD. TRIB. etc.
Cwnd arms, furnace r., windlass to l. H. 169. Types Fis.
91, Fon. 6408. Nearly fine, small nicks, obv. edge dent. 44.   1

828   1789 Another, from same dies as last. V. fine. Æ. 44.   1

829   1790 * REGI * MAX * CAROLO * III etc. Bust of the King
and Queen conjoined r. ℞ Minerva setd before book-
case. H. 170, Fis. 99, Fon. 6417. Fine ; scratches on rev.
Æ. 48.   1

830   Another, from same dies as last. A few scratches. Æ gilt. 48.   1

831   **Oaxaca.** 1789 CARLOS * IV * REY * etc. Spanish arms
bet. pillars. ℞ PROCLAMADO. EN LA. CIUDAD DE OAXACA. A. .
5 line ins. within wreath. H. 174, Fis. 480. V. fine. 28½.   1

832   Another, from same dies as last. V. good. Æ. 28½. Also
one with slightly dif. obv., less punctuations, and periods instead of rosettes. V. fair, holed. Æ. 28.   2

833   **Orizaba.** 1790 A * CARLOS * IV * REY * etc. Head r. by
Gil. ℞ EN * SU * PROCLAMACION * etc. DE ORIZAVA *
Arms of city and Spanish arms on eagle, crown above. H.
175, Fis. 596. V. fine. 39.   1

834   1790. Cwnd Spanish arms bet. pillars. ℞ EN SU PROCLAMA-
CION In field, LA MUI | LEAL VILLA | DE ORIZAVA.—EN II.
ABRIL | DE 1790 H. 176, Fon. 7044. Abt perfect, rare. 34½.   1

835   1790. Another, from same dies as last, with correct, fancy
edge. Perfect. Æ. 35.   1

836   1790. Others, type as last. H. 177. Abt perfect. 28. H.
178. Fine. 17.   2

837   **Puebla.** 1790 * A * CARLOS * IV * REY * CATOLICO * Bust
r. by *Gil.* ℞ EN * SU * FELIZ * PROCLAMACION LA * CIU-
DAD * DE * LOS * ANGELES City arms between branches
crossed, cwn above. H. 188, Fis. 526, Fon. type 6956. V.
good a few light nicks. Æ. 48.   1

838   1790 CAROLO * IV etc. Cwnd Spanish arms bet. pillars. ℞
S * P * Q * | ANGELOPOLIT * | IN * | PROCLAMATIONE · |
etc. in 7 lines. H. 190, Fis. 529, Fon. 6957. Edge plain.
About perfect. 40.   1

839   1790 Type of last. Periods for punctuations. H. 191, Fis.
528, Fon. 6958. Edge plain. 28, also size 22, same design
without ornate circle on rev. Very fine, brilliant.   2

840 (1790) IN * DIE etc. CAROLI * QUARTI * Bust *r.* ℞ ANGEL-
OPOLITANA etc. Vase with flowers in shield surmtd. by
mitre and crossed keys. H. 194, Fis. 524, Fon. 6955.
Nearly perfect. Æ. 42.   1

841 1790 CAROLVS IV . REX CATHOLICVS . coarsely engraved bust *r.*
below, *Sanches.* ℞ Caroli IV Hisp | et Ind . Reg Proclama |
tio Augusta Angelop. in | Nova Hisp . die XVII | Janva .
MDccLxxxx. | A. D. Ignatio Maria de | Victoria, Salasat
Frias | et Moctesuma Magno | Ue Xillifero. Not in H.
V. g., small hole above head. Exceptionally rare. 40. Plate.   1

842 Queretaro. 1790 Carlos * IV * etc. Bust *r.* ℞ PROC-
LAMADO * EN * LA * NOBLE etc. Mars, advancing *l.*, holds
shield in *l.* hand, standard in *r.* H. 198. Types Fis. 542,
Fon. 6964. Fine. Æ gilt. 45.   1

843 Real del Catorce. (1791) * D * D * CAROLI * IIII * etc.
Bust *r.* ℞ SED NOS CEDAMUS AMORI ' and inscrip. in 7
lines. 8-ptd star and rays above. H. 202, Fis. 564, Fon.
6974. Very fine, partly bright. Æ. 41.   1

844 (1791) Legend sim. to last. Cwnd arms of Spain within order
chain. ℞ Sim. to last. H. 203. Type Fis. 563, Fon. 6975.
About perfect, rare. 34.   1

845 (1791) Another from same dies as last. Perfect. Æ, with
correct edge. 35.   1

846 (1791) Another, same type as preceding. H. 204. About perfect. 28.   1

847 San Luis Potosi. 1790 * CARLOS * IIII * REY * etc. Bust
r., sim. to 843. ℞ * EN * SU * PROCLAMACION * etc. City
arms in cwnd shield, separate ANO—1790 H. 206 (40 Pesetas). Fine. 41.   1

848 1790. Another, from same dies as last. V. fine. Æ gilt. 41½.   1

849 1790 A CARLOS IV. REY etc. Cwnd arms of Spain within circle.
℞ EN SU | PROCLAMACION. | LA | CIUDAD | DE SAN LUIS | PO-
TOSI · | A · D · 1790 · H. 207, Fon. 6979. Nearly perfect. 34.   1

850 1790. Others of same type. H. 208, 209, 210. Sizes 28. 22,
17. Nearly perfect.   3

851 San Miguel el Grande. 1791. Obv. same as 814. ℞
PROCLAMA° * EN * S * MIGUEL Arms in oval shield surmounted by helmet *l.* H. 212, Fis. 441, Fon. 6896. V.
fine. Æ. 46.   1

852 **Sombrerete.** 1791 CAROL † IIII † DEI † GRATIA etc. Bust
     r. ℞ JURA * DE * SOMBRERETE etc. Mountain of rock
     within ornate circle. H. 220 (40 Pesetas). Very fine, rare.
     40.   1

853 1791. Obv. same as 843. ℞ Same as last. H. 221, type Fis.
     653, Fon. 7066. Fine. Æ gilt. 40.   1

854 1791 Carolus * IIII * Die * etc. Cwnd arms of Spain. ℞
     Type of 852. Mountain within plain circle. Circle of large
     dots around borders. H. 222, Fis. 748. Fine, a few nicks.
     Rare. 39.   1

855 **Tabasco.** 1790 * CARLOS * IV * REY etc. Head *l.* ℞
     PROCLAMADO * POR EL LICENCIADO | D * LORENZO * etc.
     in 7 lines. H. 224. Very fine, brilliant. Exceedingly rare.
     28½.   1

856 **Valladolid.** 1791 CARLOS † IIII † REY etc. Bust *r.* Ribbon
     and order directly below. ℞ PROCLAMADO * EN * LA CIU-
     DAD * * etc. POR * SU * ALFEREZ * R * D * JOSE BERNADO
     etc. in dbl. legend. Three busts in oval shld. cwnd. H. 227.
     Type, Fis. 471, Fon. 6929. Fine, very rare. 44.   1

857 1790 Another from same dies as last. Fine. Æ. 44.   1

858 1790 CARLOS * IIII * REY * etc. Spanish arms in round shld.
     ℞ Por * Su * | Alfrez * R * D * | Jose * | Bernado *
     Foncerrada * in field. H. 228. Fine. Very rare. 28.   1

859 **Vera Cruz.** 1789 * CAROLUS * IV * etc. Bust *r.*, sim. to
     810. Signed *Geroni Antonio Gil.* ℞ NOV * VERA CRUZ *
     PROCLAM * etc. Arms shield on base. H. 229, Fon. 7046.
     V. fine, a few light scratches, rare. 40.   1

860 1789. Obv. from same die as last. ℞ Sim. with * Sebastian
     * Perez * H. 231. V. fine and rare. 40.   1

861 **Zacatecas.** n.d. * In * Proclamacione * Caroli * etc.
     Bust *r.* ℞ ZACATECANAE * URBIS * etc. Cwnd arms in oval
     shld. H. 232 (40 Pesetas), type Fis. 613, Fon. 7078. Fine,
     holed above head, and a few small nicks. 41.   1

FERDINAND VII. Proclaimed Heir 1790; *succeeded* 19 *March,* 1808.

862 **Chiapa.** 1808 Fernando. VIII. etc. Cwnd arms of Spain
     below 2 R(eals). ℞ Pro | clamado | en Ciudad | R. de
     Chia | pa. Ano | 1808 Wrth. Another of same type for 1
     Real. H. 10 and 9. Nearly fine. 27, 20.   2

863 Guadalajara. 1809 FERDINANDUS ' VII ' SUMMO Bust *r.*
℞ Trident . Guadalax . Colleg . etc. Mars and Indian
Princess richly robed, stdg. Ex., FIDES | HISP. | FIDES | IND.
H. 11. V. fine ; loop removed. Æ gilt. Slightly oval. 37
x 41.   1

864 Jalapa. 1808 Ferdinand ' VII ' etc. Cwnd arms of Spain
within dotted circle. ℞ En su Proclamacion. In field, LA
VILLA | DE XALAPA | EN 29 ' DE SE | PTIEMBRE | DE 1808
H. 23, Fis. 604, Fon. 7050. Nearly perfect. 33.   1

865 1808 Another, same type. Nearly fine. 27.   1

866 Mexico. 1808 A ' Fernando ' VII ' etc. Bust facing slightly
r. ℞ EN SU EXALTACION AL TRONO. LA CIUDAD DE MEXICO '
Indian princess and eagle sup. cwnd arms of the city. H.
29 (40 Pesetas), Fis. 126, (Fon. 6474 rev.) V. fine. 44.   1

867 1808 Another as last, slight nicks on edge. Æ. 43. Also
bust in profile *r.* ℞ As last. H. 30. V. fine. Æ, silvered. 44.   2

868 1808 Fernando ' VII ' etc. Crowned arms of Spain. ℞ Pro-
clama | do en Mexico | a 13' | de Agost' | del año de | * 1808 *
Wreath, circle of large dots around borders. H. 32, Fis. 125,
Fon. 6478. Fine. 39½.   1

869 1808. Another, type as last. 2 Real size. Fine. 27.   1

870 1809 * FERDINANDUS VII BORBONIVS etc. Bust *l.* ℞ POES etc.
ELOQVENT etc. Minerva setd before book-case. H. 34, type
Fis. 134. Very fine, rare. 49.   1

871 1809. Another, from same dies as last. Nearly perfect, partly
bright. Æ. 49.   1

872 1808 FERDIN . VII . HISPANIARUM etc. Bust *l.* ℞ PRO SOLIO
— REG. SANCT. ILD. MEX. COLL. Hearts encircled by chains.
Die projecting loop, oval floral attachment depending from
bar. H. 35, Fis. 130, Fon. 6476. Fine, a few light scratches.
Æ gilt, oval, 37 x 45.   1

873 1808 FERDIN . VII . HISP . etc. Draped bust *r.* head laur. ℞
INTACTAE FIDEI | MONINENTUM | etc. MEX. ACAD. | in 6 lines.
H. 36, Fis. 128, Fon. 6475. Die proj. loop. V. fine, a few
slight nicks. Æ gilt, oval, 38 x 46.   1

874 1809 FERDINANDO VII CAPTIVO etc. Bust *r.*, by *Guerrero.* ℞
COLLEGIUM MEXICANUM. A General, Pope and Cardinal
setd, behind them a mantle depending from crown. Fis.
140, not in H. or Fon. Abt perfect, v. rare. Oval, 37 x 45.   1

815 1809.   Another, from same dies as last.   Holed by loop at-
attached.   Not in Fis., H. or Fon.   Good, extremely rare.
Æ gilt.   1

876 Oaxaca. 1808 FERNANDO VII . etc.   Cwnd arms of Spain
bet. pillars.   ℞ PROCLAMADO · EN LA CIUDAD etc.   Lion in
cwnd shld.   H. 42, Fis. 482, Fon. 6949.   V. fine, bril. 27.   1

877 1808.   Another, sim.   ℞ POR EL | ALFEREZ. R. | D. FELIPE |
ORDONEZ. | DIAZ.   Wrth.   H. 43, Fis. 481, Fon. 6950.   V.
fine. 27.   1

878 1809 FERDINAND · VII · REDEAS etc.   Bust *l.*   ℞ SANCTÆ AN-
TEQUERENSE (Oaxaca) COLLEG · UTRIQ. etc.   Minerva setd *l.*
beside column, holds cwn, from which depends a chain.   Not
in H., Fis. 135, Fon. 6284.   Nearly perfect, rare.   Æ gilt,
oval, 52 x 62.   Plate.   1

This piece (of which there is but one in the sale) through error also appears as lot
647. It will be sold as lot 878.

879 Parras. 1809 Ferdinandus · VII · Rex Maximus etc.   Bust
r.   ℞ EXPECTATISSIMO NOSTRO | FERDINANDO · VII : | etc.,
in 8 lines, over which hangs a garland.   H. 45.   Fine.   Æ
gilt ; holed above head.   Rare. 40.   1

880 1809 Fernando · VII · etc.   Bust sim. to last.   ℞ LOS | MORA-
DORES | DE PARRAS . | EN DESAHOGO | etc. in 6 lines.   Gar-
land as last.   H. 46.   Fine, v. rare. 28.   1

881 Pasquaro. 1808 Fernando · VII · etc.   ℞ PROCLAMADO |
EN PASQUARO | EN 14 · DE OCTUBRE DEL ANO | DE 1808 within
wreath.   H. 47, Fon. 6950 (61 Mks).   Fine, rare. 39.   1

882 1808 Type as last.   Fine, very rare. 27.   1

883 1808 FERDIN VII etc.   MERITO EXOPTATISSIMUS Bust *r.*   ℞
INTER TRIBULOS etc. ANGELOP, ECCLA   Vase with flowers.
H. 52, Type Fis. 530, Fon. 6961.   V. fine and rare. 36 x 42.   1

884 Puebla. 1809 FERNANDO VII · A GALLIS CAPTO ·   Bust *r.* and
closely imitating 874, but unsigned.   ℞ PERFIDIAM FIDE
etc.   Angels carrying cathedral (city arms).   H. 51, Fon.
6963.   Die projecting loop.   Very fine, rare.   Æ.   Oval.
39 x 47.   1

885 1809 AMOR MEUS FERDINANDVS EST   Bust *r.* on a heart.   ℞
REGAL. COLLEG | A VEN. PALAFAXIO | etc. in 6 lines within
wreath.   Die proj. loop with branches.   H. 54 (40 Pesetas),
Fon. 6962.   About perfect.   V. rare. 39 x 48.   1

886 1809 FERDINANDO VII · EXSPECTATISSIMO CAESARI Bust *r.* ℞
    CAROLINI | ANGELOP . COLLEG. | etc. in 7 lines. Die proj.
    ornamented loop. Fis. 531 ; not in H. or Fon. Nearly fine,
    very rare. Æ gilt. 44.   1

887 **Quautla de Amilpas.** 1809 Fernando . VII . etc. Cwnd
    arms of Spain in round shield. ℞ POR EL | ALFEREZ | REAL
    DON | etc. in 7 lines. Wreath. H. 58, Fis. 540, Fon. 6738.
    Nearly fine. 27.   1

888 **Queretaro.** 1808 FERNANDO * VII * etc. Cwnd arms of
    Spain bet. pillars. ℞ PROCLAMADO | EN QUERETARO etc.
    ANO . 1808 | * 4 R * Wreath. H. 60, Fis. 544. V. fine.
    34.   1

889 **San Francisco Yxtlahuaca.** 1809 Fernando · VII · etc.
    Bust *r.* ℞ PROCLAMADO | EN LA VILLA DE | S. FRANC°̣ YXTLA-
    HUACᴬ | etc. in 7 lines, draped with a garland. H. 66 (45
    Pesetas). V. fine, rare. 40.   1

890 1809. Another, type of last. H. 67, Fis. 336, Fon. 6741.
    About perfect. 28.   1

891 **San Luis Potosi.** 1808 FERNANDO VII · etc. Bust *r.* in high
    relief. ℞ Type of 847. H. 68 (40 Pesetas), Fis. 552, Fon.
    6981. Fine, a few slight dents, very rare. 41.   1

892 **San Nicolas de Actopan.** 1808 PROCLAMADO EN S. NICOLAS
    ACTOPAN etc. Cwnd arms of Spain bet. branches. ℞ FER-
    DINANDO VII | GRANDIBVS GENTIVM | etc. in 6 lines. H. 72,
    Fis. 334. Fine, rare. 40.   1

893 1808. Another, type of preceding. H. 73, Fis. 333. Fine. 27. 1

894 1808. Another, with a rev. die differing in all minor details.
    Not noted by H. Fine, holed near edge. 27.   1

895 **Santiago de Tuxtla.** 1809 Fernando · VII · From same
    die as 881. ℞ PROCLAMADO | EN LA VILLA DE | SANTIAGO
    TUXTLA | etc. | DEL VALLE DE OA | XACA etc. in 8 lines. H.
    82. Good, very rare. 39.   1

896 **Tacuba.** 1808 Fernando VII. etc. Obv. same as 887. ℞
    PROCLAMADO | EN LA VILLA DE TA- | CUBA etc. in 10 lines.
    H. 83, Fis. 360, Fon. 6742. Fine. 27.   1

897 **Toluca.** 1809 Fernando. VII. etc. Pierced heart in cwnd
    shld. ℞ ANO | DE 1809. | PROCLAMADO EN LA | CIUD. DE
    TOLUCA etc. in 9 lines. H. 85, Fis. 362. Nearly perfect,
    very rare. 33.   1

898 **Valladolid.** 1808 Bust *r*. ℞ PROCLAMADO ' EN LA CIUDA '
etc. POR LA NOBI- LISIMA ' CIUDAD Type of 856, letters in
legend much larger. H. 87. Fine, very rare. 42.   1

899 **Vera Cruz.** 1808 Bust *r*., sim. to 884. ℞ A very good copy
of 859. H. 88, Fis. 600, Fon. 7047. Fine, numerous light
nicks, rare. 39.   1

900 **Zacatecas.** 1808 Bust *r*. ℞ PROCLAMADO EN LA CIUD^P
DE ZACAT^S POR SUS LEALES COMERC^S Y MINEROS. City arms
in oval shld cwnd. H. 90 (40 Pesetas), Type Fis. 614. V.
good ; a few scratches. 41.   1

901 **Zamora.** 1808 Fernando VII * etc. Cwnd arms of Spain
in round shld. ℞ POR EL ALF? | R! DON LAZARO | MORALES
etc. in 6 lines. H. 91 (40 Pesetas), Fis. 473. V. fine and
v. rare. 31.   1

902 1808 Another, type of preceding, but a size not found in H.,
Fis. or Fon. V. fine, brilliant, exceptionally rare. 39.   1

CENTRAL AMERICA.
FERDINAND VI.

903 **Guatemala.** 1747 FERD ' VI ' etc. Bust *r*. ℞ GUAT . IN .
EIUS . PROCLAMACIONE Horse *l*. above two mts. H. 42, B.
345. Holed and much worn, yet every part of type and
legend remains. Rare. 33.   1

904 1747 Another of same design, differing in all minor details.
Flames issue from mt. *l*. ; sword points to s in EIUS. Not in
H. Very fine and extremely rare. 31.   1

905 1747 Same design. H. 43. Good, holed. 23½. Another still
smaller. H. 44. V. good, twice holed near edge. Rare. 17½.   2

CHARLES III.

906 **Guatemala.** 1760 CAROLUS ' III ' etc. Bust *r*. ℞ Legend
same as 903. Mtd horseman *r;* flames from mt. *r*. H. 65,
Fon. 7184. Good. Rare. 34.   1

907 1760 Similar. H. 62. Nearly fine, holed. 27.   1

908 1760 Others sim. PROCLAMATIO Type, H. 63. Good, holed.
20½. PROCLAMATIONE Type, H. 64. Fine, holed. 16½.   2

CHARLES IV.

909 **Guatemala.** 1789 CAROL . IV . etc. Draped bust *r*., below,
P. G. A. ℞ S. P. Q. G. PROCLAMAT . 18 NOV. A. 1789 ; mts
and horseman *l*. in shield. Types, H. 145, Cat. 4, 4a. V.
fine, brilliant. Rare. 34½.   1

910 1789 Similar. Naked bust, P. G. A. Mts. and horseman are
     in a beaded circle. Type, H. 146. V. fine. 29.   1

911 1789 Similar bust in coat with Order and ribbon. P. G. A. on
     truncation. ℞ Mts and horseman *l.* Type H. 148. Very
     good. 21. Salvador. 1789 Naked bust *r.* ℞ SALUADOR |
     EN IND. etc. Mountain. A var. of H. 214. Good, holed
     and broken through edge.   2

FERDINAND VII.

912 **Guatemala.** 1808 * A * FERNANDO * VII * etc. Bust *r.*
     by *P. Garcia Guirre.* ℞ * LAM. N. YL CIUDAD DE GUATE-
     MALA etc. Arms in cwnd shld on palm branches crossed.
     H. 12 (75 Pesetas). Very fine, holed near edge, extremely
     rare. 44.   1

913 1808 * FERNANDO * VII * ANO * I * DE SU REINA * Bust *r.*
     ℞ GUATEMALA ANO 284 etc. Arms in cwnd shld sep. 2 — R.
     H. 13, Cat. 4, 11. V. fine, brill. 28.   1

914 1808 Sim. to last. REYN 5 and 6 ptd stars. ℞ From same
     die as last. H. 14. V. fine, brill. 28.   1

915 1808 FERNANDO · VII · H. 15 ; and FERDIN . HISP . VII . Type
     H. 16. Reverses from same die. Fine. 21.   2

916 **Leon de Nicaragua.** 1808 Bust *r.* From same die as first
     pc in last lot. ℞ PROCLA · EN · LA · N · C · DE · LEON etc.
     Lion *r.* in shld sep. 1 — R. H. 27, Cat. 4, 129, Fon. 7375.
     V. fine. 20.   1

917 **Olancho.** 1808 * A * FERNANDO * VII * EL * AMADO *
     Bust *r.* ℞ SIEMPRE * FLORECIENTE * COMO * LA * PALMA *
     Palm tree. EL . BATA — LLION . DE | OLAN — CHO : Bor-
     ders of leaves. H. 44 (50 Pesetas). V. fine, ex. rare. 40.   1

918 **Quesaltenango.** 1808 Bust and legend sim. to 913, periods
     for punctuations. ℞ QUESAL– | * TENANGO * | etc. | . 2 .
     R. in 5 lines, border of fleurs-de-lis. H. 62. Fine and rare.
     27.   1

919 **San Salvador.** 1808. Obv. from same die as 913. ℞ Pro-
     clamado en la. N. C. de S. Salvador. etc. Mountain within
     circle. H. 74, Cat. 4, 77. Fine, rare. 27.   1

920 1808 · FERNANDO · VII etc. INDIAS (last four letters beneath
     bust). ℞ Proclamado . en . S. Salvador . de . G . Mt.
     within beaded circle. H. 76, Cat. 4, 76, Fon. 7464. Fine. 21.   1

921 **Santa Ana la Grande.** 1808 FERNANDO . VII . etc. Bust
sim. to preceding. ℞ Santa Ana Grande . en G . In field,
POR | SU LEAL | etc. ·I·R· in 5 lines. H. 77, Cat. 4, 82, Fon.
7472. Fine. 21.   1

922 **Truxillo.** 1808 Bust sim. to 918. REY . DE . ESP . E . IND .
℞ PROCLA . EN . LA . C . DE . etc. Arms of the city in cwnd
shld, sep. .2.—.R. H. 86. Fine, very rare. 28.   1

SOUTH AMERICA.

CHARLES III.

923 **Buenos Aires.** 1760 CAROLVS · III · etc. in large letters.
Bust *r.* ℞ PROCLAMATVS · BON · AER · Two ships sailing
towards each other, eagle above. (Arms of the city.) H. 52,
B. 450. V. fine orig. cast. V. rare. 36.   1

924 **Lima.** 1760 Bust *r.* within corded circle ; date in legend.
℞ OPTIMO PRINC ✿ PUBL. ✿ etc. Dbl hd eagle cwnd bet.
pillars. H. 71, B. 469, Cat. 4, 512. Fine. 38.   1

925 1760 Another, from same dies as last, struck on a thin planchet. Fine. 37½.   1

926 **Quito.** 1760 CAROLVS III HISPA · REX. Bust *l.* resting on
two globes, star behind. ℞ VTRAQVE EN QUITO 176. Cwnd
arms of Spain. Not in H. A fine orig. cast. 34. Plate.   1

CHARLES IV.

927 **Cartagena.** 1789 Carol ✳ IV ✳ etc. Bust *r.* ℞ PROCLA-
MATUS ✳ CARTAG ✳ YND ✳ Lions sup. cross, crowned. H.
126. Fine, rare. 34.   1

928 **Chile.** 1789 CAROLUS IV . etc. IMPERAT AUGUST. Bust *r.*
By *Nazaul.* Ex. 1789. ℞ OPTIMO IMPERAT etc. Q. CHILEN-
SIS. Lion *l.* in cwnd shld. H. 129. V. fine, bril. 43.   1

929 1789 Obv. from same die as last. ℞ HIGINIUS PRÆFECT. CHIL.
PROCLAMAVIT etc. Two Indians in field, one with bow and
arrow, the other holds lance. H. 130. V. fine, v. rare, brilliant. 43.   1

930 **Cochabamba.** 1789 CAROLUS ✳ IV ✳ etc. Bust *r.*, large hd.
℞ MAG ✳ CIUIT ✿ HEC ✳ etc. COCHABAMBA in monogram.
Lion *l.* in shld, within frame containing nine human heads.
H. 132, Fon. 9748. Fine, extremely rare. 40.   1

931 Cumana. 1789 CAROLVS 4 · D · G HISPAN · REX Bust *r*. ℞
D · ANDTESFRS · POR · CVMANA In field, TOVR in large mon.
Not in H. A fine orig. cast, exceptionally rare. 28½. Plate. 1

932 Florida Oriental. 1789 Bust *r*. with usual titles. ℞ LA
FLOR.ᴬ ORIENTAL PER ZESPED^S PROCLAM.ᵀᵁᴿ In field, a star-
fish ; above, a castle ; below a lion rampant *l*. H. 133. V.
fine, extremely rare. 34. 1

A piece of the same design, though from very different dies, was in my sale of April
12, 1897, and I attributed it to East Florida (a part of the present State of Florida),
under Spanish domain, at the time when it was issued. Herrera has nothing to say on
this point, as it is arranged in its alphabetical order under "América Española"; therefore, he escapes further criticism. Mr. Betts prefers Uruguay for its home, and gives his
reasons as follows : — " So attributed because it is so entirely different in design, style of
work, etc., from anything emanating from the West Indies or their neighborhood ; because
the region in which the town of Florida (a place of some importance about fifty miles
nearly north from Montevideo), is situated, was for nearly two hundred years known as
the *Banda Oriental*, and was at the accession of Charles IV, in the possession of Spain ;
and because it would seem entirely natural that it should be so called by way of distinc-
tion. Herrera calls the device on the reverse a " Sea Star " (Estrella de Mer), by which I
suppose he means a *Star Fish.*

933 Huancavelica. 1790 CAROL · IV · DEI GRA · etc. Bust *r*.
℞ ME · FERE · JAM TOTUM · etc. Stone pyramid surmounted
by orb and cross. H. 153, Cat. 4, 625, Fon. 9244. Thick
planchet. V. fine, some faint scratches. 37. 1

934 1790 Another, from same dies as last, on a thin planchet. *V.
small* punch with letters E L H stamped below bust. Fine,
brilliant. 36½. 1

935 La Plata. 1789 Titles and bust, wonderfully like 930, punctuations *above* line of bottom of letters. Legend ends in
mon. of La Plata. ℞ ✸ OPTIMO ✸ PRINC ✸ PUBLICE ✸ etc.
Dbl-headed eagle bet. pillars, mt. at either side, resting on
four castles. H. 155. Fine, rare. 40. 1

936 Lima. 1789 Cwnd arms of Spain, within Order chain. ℞
PUBLIC ✚ FIDELIT ✚ etc. Dbl-hded eagle cwnd, bet. pillars.
H. 156, Cat. 4, 512, Fon. 8942. Fine. 37. 1

937 Popayan. 1790 CAROL ✸ IV ✸ D ✸ G ✸ etc. Bust *r*. ℞
PROCLAMATUS ✸ IN ✸ CIVIT ✸ POPAIANENSI Two mts., below, a village. H. 186, Cat. 4, 387, Fon. 8218. Fine. 32½. 1

938 Potosi. 1789 Bust *r*., a still closer copy of 903 ; date a trifle
further from bust, mon. at end of legend. ℞ OPTIMO ✳
PRINC ✳ etc. Dbl-hded eagle cwnd, on summit of mt., bet.
pillars. H. 187. Fine, rare. 40. 1

939 **Santa Fe de Bogota.** 1789 . CAROL . IV . D . G . etc. Bust
r. ℞ SANTA FIDES FIRMAT etc. Eagle in cwnd shld. H.
215. Nearly fine, holed above hd near edge, v. rare. 33.   1

940 **Tarma.** 1789 Obv. from same die as 936. ℞ PUBLIC *
FIDELIT * etc. In field, VIVA | EL | REY | GAL | VEZ | TAR |
MA * H. 225. V. good, extremely rare. 36.   1

FERDINAND VII.

941 **Buenos Ayres.** 1808 * A FERNANDO VII * REY etc. Bust
l. By *Arrabal.* ℞ * JURA ᐧ LA ᐧ CIUDAD DE ᐧ BUENOS ᐧ
AYRES ᐧ etc. Female setd beside shield with city arms, receives warrior. H. 7, Cat. 4, 1084, Fon. 10062. V. fine, brilliant. 43½.   1

942 **Caracas.** 1812 FERNᴼ VII . DEI D . LAS ESPANAS . Bust r.
℞ DOMᴼ D . MONTEUᴱ LE PROCᴼ EN CARˢ CEP . 24ᴰ 1812 Lion
l. holds shield with city arms. H. 8, Fon. 7973. Gd, holed,
very rare. 31½.   1

943 **Colonia** (n.d.) V.A in mon., cross-bar of A extending, makes
it possible to interpret VII below, F. 7ᴼ ℞ COLᴬ beneath
monstrance. H. 93. V. fine orig. cast ; exceptionally rare.
30. Plate.   1

Regarding this piece, Mr. Betts observes : — " I so attribute this because the name
originally was ' *Colonia di Sancti Spiritus.*' The *monstrance*, as a device on the reverse
seems to point in the same direction as being entirely appropriate, and the abbreviation
Colᵃ would be a very likely abbreviation for Colonia. Herrera classes it as uncertain
(*incierta*) but follows Rivadicira in suggesting ' *Santiago de Compostella*' as probable."

944 **Honda.** 1808 Fernando VII . Rey etc. In field, MAGNO IN
ORTU | MAJOR IN etc. in 4 lines. ℞ PROCLAMACION DE LA
UILLA DE HONDA Dbl hd eagle cwnd on arched bridge. H.
22. V. fine, brilliant, rare. 36.   1

945 **La Plata.** 1808 Ferdinando . VII . etc. Lion beside castle,
tramples on dbl hd eagle. ℞ Optimo . Princ . etc. Arms
sim. to 935. H. 26. Fine, holed, rare. 38½.   1

946 **Lima.** 1808 Ferdinandus VII. Bust r. by *Soto.* ℞ Publicæ . Fidelitatis . Juram . Limæ . Dbl hd eagle cwnd bet.
pillars ; below, ABASCAL | 13 . OCTOB . | 1808 H. 28, Cat. 4,
627, Fon. 8968. Nearly perfect, rare. 38½.   1

947 **Montevideo.** 1808 FERNAD VII ᐧ SP ᐧ ET ᐧ IND REX. Bust
facing. ℞ PROCLAMATUS ᐧ IN MONTEVIDEO 1808 In field,
a castle ; above, FERNANDO . VII . on label. A bold orig.
cast. Not in H. Fine, uncommonly rare. 36½. Plate.   1

948 **New Granada.** 1808 AUGUSTA | PROCLAMACION | DEL N. R.
D. G. POR | FERNANDO . VII | etc. in 6 lines. ℞ REI DE
ESPA etc. Cwnd arms of Spain. H. 39, Cat. 4, 394, Fon. 8047.
Fine. 26½.   I

949 **New Santander.** 1809 FERNANDO * VII * REY * etc.
Cwnd arms of Spain bet. pillars. ℞ PROCLAMADO | EN LA
CAPITAL | DEL NUEBO SAN | TANDER etc. in 6 lines. Wreath.
H. 40. Nearly perfect; very rare. 40.   I

950 1809 Another, type of preceding. H. 41. Nearly perfect;
rare. 27.   I

951 **Popayan.** 1808 FERDINANDUS VII * PREDILECTUS HISP *
ET IND * REX Bust *r*. ℞ PROCLAMATUS * etc. POPAIANEN-
SI * Two mts. behind village. H. 49, Fon. 8218. Very
good. 32½.   I

952 **Potosi.** 1808 POTOSI * | PRO | FERNANDO VII * | ANNO |
1808 ℞ Double-headed eagle on summit of mountain
between pillars, type of 938. H. 50, Fon. 9391. Fine.
40.   I

953 1808 Another as last, with slightly differing rev. Potosi very
high in wreath. A var. unnoticed by H., Fon. 9392. Fine.
40. Plate.   I

954 **Puno.** 1808 FERNANDO · VII · D.G. OPTATO · PRINC · JURAT *
City arms in cwnd shld on crossed cannon, etc. ℞ PUNO|
HISPANIARVM | etc. in 5 lines. H. 55. Fine, holed, very
rare. Æ gilt. 40.   I

955 1808 Another, type as last, but superior in workmanship. H.
56, Fon. 9251. About perfect, extremely rare. 26.   I

956 1808 Another still smaller; as well executed as last. H. 57.
Very fine and rare. 20.   I

957 **Santa Fe de Bogota.** 1808 EN AMOR DE FERNANDO VII
REY etc. Bust *r*. ℞ EL COMERCIO DE SANTA FE etc.
Two lions supporting crowned cross; emblems of commerce below. H. 79, Cat. 4, 390, Fon. 8046. Very fine
and rare. 40½.   I

958 **Tarma.** 1808 FERDINANDUS · VII · D · G · etc. Bust *r*. ℞
PUBLICÆ FIDELITATIS JURAMENTUM TARMAE. In field, URRU-
TIA | etc. in 3 lines. Lion above. H. 84, Cat. 4, 667, Fon.
9259. Nearly fine. 33.   I

DECORATIONS AND ORDERS.

958a Bronze eagle, wings spread, white neck, in centre within white oval. Senators present sword to Cincinnatus at his home, his wife stdg at the door. ℞ A soldier discharging a piece of artillery: suspended from ring by band of green leaves. Ribbon. About perfect. 27 x 40.   1

This was undoubtedly an issue by the Society of the Cincinnati, yet it differs materially from any I find described.

959 Cuba. 1871 AMADEO I° REY ESPANA A LOS VOLUNTARIOS DE LA ISLA DE CUBA Head *r.* ℞ DEFENSORES etc. Two pillars, against each rests a shld. with arms, depending from crown. Ring, ribbon and buckle. Nearly perfect. Æ. 30 x 38.   1

Amadeo I to the Volunteers of the Island of Cuba for the defence of National honor and integrity in 1871.

960 1873 ESPANA | AL | VALIENTE EJERCITO | etc., in 8 lines. ℞ CAMPANA | DE | CUBA Spain setd. on stone against pillar, lozenge form, around which branches bend ; depending from crown. Ring and ribbon. About perfect. Æ. 31 x 37.   1

960a Flag of three blue and two white horizontal stripes, with one white star on red, on field with palm-tree and plant within shield encircled by wreath, clasp pin on back. Fine. Æ gilt. 26.   1

961 Haiti. Order of Faustin 1st FAUSTIN IER FONDATEUR — 1849 on blue. Bust *l.* in gilt on 7 ptd white star. Wreath in green encircles points. ℞ Crown in gilt on red. Loop from crown with ring. Some enamel slightly chipped ; otherwise fine. 42.   1

962 Another of the same Order, differently and better executed. FAUSTIN IER EMPEREUR D'HAITI ℞ Eagle on crossed canon on 8-armed cross in red and blue alternating ; crown and ring as last. Some enamel chipped ; otherwise fine. 43.   1

963 Puerto Rico. ESCMO AYUNTAMIENTO DE SAN JUAN DE PUERTO-RICO. Paschal lamb *r.* in oval within wrth. ℞ Oval arms shld within Order chain. Wreath enclosing oblong, octagon shell 39 x 55, depending from cwn, with ring. Very fine. Gilt.   1

964 Mexico. 1821 SE DISTINGIO EN TEPEACA on white band, gilt
      castle and house on rock within, on blue field. ℞ 20 21 Y
      22 | DE ABRIL | DE 1821 all on white cross, ends joined by
      gilt wreath, depending from inscribed bar, held by eagle.
      Portion of enamel on bar is gone, otherwise fine. 41.   1

965 1856 COMBATIO | POR LA INTEGRI | DAD DEL TERRI | TORIO
      NACIO | NAL on white centre. ℞ TEXAS —EN 1836, all on
      white star, arrow pts in angles, depending from gilt and
      green wreath, with ribbon. Fine, rare and highly interest-
      ing. 36.   1

966 1847 COMBATIO POR EL TERRITORIO NACL. on white, with gilt
      edge, sabres crossed within. ℞ 8 12 Y 13 | DE | SETIEMBRE
      | DE 1847 All encircled by gilt and green wrth, looped to
      gilt eagle and ring. Fine. 14.   1

967 1861–67 PREMIO — AL PATRIOTISMO In field, COMBATIO | A
      LA INTERVENCION | FRANCESA Y SUS | ALIADOS DESDIE | 1861-
      HASTA 1867 White, on red cross, ends encircled by green
      wreath. ℞ SALVO | LA | INDEPENDENCIA | etc. Red cross,
      rays in angles, depending from eagle. Ribbon. Fine. Silver.
      37.   1

968 1863 DEFENDIO PUEBLA DE ZARAGOZA on white band, gilt eagle
      on red field within, all on gilt and green cross, depending
      from bar and ribbon. Fine. Gold. 14 x 15.   1

969 1863 DEFENDIO A PUEBLA | DE | ZARAGOZA | EN | 1863 | CON-
      TRA | EL | E(JERCI)TO FRANCES on black oval, circled with
      red, in centre of cross of gilt, bordered with green. ℞ The
      Mexican eagle on white. Loop and suspender, all inserted
      on silver. Oval, 38 x 46.   1

A military decoration for special service, designed for the concealment of despatches.
Of unusual interest.

970 n.d. Same design as 967. COOPERO | A LA | DEFENSA DE LA |
      REPUBLICA | CONTRA | EL EJERCITO | FRANCES White, on
      red cross, gilt and green wreath, gilt rays, loop, suspender
      and ribbon. Fine. 45.   1

971 Royal Am. Order of Isabella the Catholic. A 4-armed, 8-ptd
      cross of gilt and red, with radiations in angles. In centre,
      A LA LEALTAD A CRISOLA etc. on white band containing
      green wreath; within, two columns and two globes. Clasp
      pin on back. Perfect. 85 between points.   1

972   A cross of the same design and composition, with F. R. in
      script, linked and crowned on blue, depending from wreath,
      with ring and ribbon.   About perfect.   45.   1

973   Another, similarly constructed, size 39 ; also miniature of same,
      size 12.   Both with ring and ribbon, and about perfect.   2

974   Order of the Eagle.   The Mexican eagle in gilt upon a plain
      gold field, jewelled in red and green settings, all on a silver
      cross, with arms ending in a lis.   In centre of rev. (in relief)
      ROTHE | JOYERO | etc. KOHLMARKT | N° 7 in 9 lines.   Pin
      and clasp.   About perfect.   94.   1

975   Another.   Eagle in gilt and bronze, holding sword and sceptre,
      depending from jewelled crown ; loop and slide, long ribbon
      with small end to tie.   Perfect, 39 x 55 (including crown).   1

976   Another of same design and composition.   Ring and ribbon.
      Green enamel out of 4 of the 13 cactus leaves, otherwise
      about perfect.   27 x 42.   1

977   Another quite as last, but silvered.   Green cactus leaves all
      perfect.   Ring and ribbon.   27 x 42.   1

978   Our Lady of Guadeloupe.   Cross of green, white and red.   RE-
      LIGION INDEPENDENCIA · UNION on oval within wreath.   Our
      Lady stdg within radiation, bound to wreath, all on 8-ptd
      star.   Pin and clasp on rev.   Æ gilt.   About perfect.
      83.   1

979   A sim. cross on wrth, in same colors.   AL | MERITO | Y | VIR-
      TUDES on rev.   Suspended from ring, with ribbon and button
      (or rosette).   Nearly perfect.   36 x 40.   Also miniature of
      same, complete with ribbon.   About perfect.   8½ x 14 (in-
      cluding eagle).   2

980   Puebla.   Two angels hold crown above cathedral in water,
      separating K — V   Oval badge, from the Fischer collection.
      V. fine.   Brass, 56 x 71.   1

981   San Carlos Cross, white and green.   San Carlos ℞ Humili-
      tas   Ring and ribbon.   V. fine.   48 x 62.   1

982   Honduras.   Order de Santa Rosa y de la Civilizacion.   In
      field, Merito | Civil.   ℞ Republica de Honduras.   In field,
      arms on gold, with white and blue flag.   Green and gilt on
      white cross cwnd with wreath, depending from wreath, with
      ring and ribbon.   Some enamel chipped away, otherwise
      fine.   44 between points.   1

983 Miniature of the preceding, with ribbon. About perfect. 11 x 14 (including wreath).   1

984 Venezuela. SIMON BOLIVAR on blue oval encircling bust *l.* in relief. ℞ The arms of Venezuela; gilt radiated border; ring, loop and long ribbon. Enamel slightly chipped in two places, otherwise v. fine. 49 x 52.   1

985 France. Legion of Honor. Napoleon Empereur des Francais. Head of Nap. I in gilt, radiated on white five-armed cross; green wreath, suspended from crown, ring and ribbon. Several points chipped, otherwise fine. 41.   1

986 Spain. Order of Maria Isabella. M. Y. in script, linked in oval, on cross, hinged from crown with ring. Fine. Æ. 26.   1
The Order was founded by Ferd. VII for the army and navy on the taking of the oath of allegiance to the infant Maria Isabella Louise, heir presumptive to the throne. Gold for officers, silver for privates.

987 Military Decoration. RECOMP. NAC. A LA CONSTANCIA EN EL SERV. MILITAR on white oval, stdg fig. in silver beside column on red field, in centre of green cross; swivel and bar inscribed CONSTANCIA. Ribbon. Abt perfect. 37 x 42.   1
Order instituted 1842, for 30 years' service.

988 Arms of Spain in centre of silver cross attached to crown. Ring and ribbon. Abt perfect. 23½ x 32.   1

989 M. M. in gilt script linked, on white in centre of red cross. ℞ Arms of Spain. Gilt borders, hinged to crown, with ring. Abt perfect. 38 x 38.   1

990 Eagle and jewels (in form only) alternate in frame forming cwn, resting on square cushion, with tassels at each corner. Abt perfect. Brass, silver-plated, 5 in. high and weighs 2¾ lbs.   1
This very interesting relic surmounted the staff carried by the Chief Magistrate of the City of Mexico, in time of Maximilian.

CABINETS (all in fine order).

991 Veneered rosewood. 9 inches high, 12 wide and 15 deep; contains 9 drawers, with numbered ivory knobs; closing door, lock and key. A superior piece of work.   1

992 Black walnut. 18¾ inches high, 15⅛ wide, 12⅝ deep; contains 18 drawers with brass knobs, and lined with velveteen. Upright bar fitted to front, with lock and key.   1

993 Black walnut. Movable display drawer fitted in case, with glass top.   1

BOOKS TREATING UPON COINS AND MEDALS.

994   Akerman, John Y. A Numismatic Manual. 420 pp. 16 plates, some illustrations. Large 8vo, cloth. London, 1840.   1

995   — An introduction to the Study of Ancient and Modern Coins. 220 pp. Illustrated. 12mo, cloth. London, 1848.   1

996   — Coins of the Romans relating to Britain. 8vo, cloth. 84 pp. 6 plates, illustrations in the text. London, 1836.   1

997   — Coins of the Romans relating to Britain. 8vo, cloth. 170 pp. 7 plates. London, 1844.   1

998   — Numismatic Illustrations of the Narrative Portions of the New Testament. 62 pp. 1 plate and engravings. 8vo, cloth. London, 1846.   1

999   — Tradesmen's Tokens, current in London and its vicinity between the years 1648 and 1672. viii and 257 pp. 8 plates. 8vo, cloth. London, 1849.   1

1000   Appleton, Wm. S. Description of a selection of Coins and Medals relating to America. 16 pp. 12 illustrations inserted (under the direction of the late Chas. I. Bushnell, whose signature the work bears on a fly-leaf). Rare ; very limited edition. Cambridge, 1870.   1

1001   Barthelemy, J. B. Nouveau Manuel Complet de Numismatique, Ancienne et Moderne. 2 vols., 12mo, and 1 vol. containing 24 plates. Small long folio. Half morocco. 920 pp. Paris, 1866.   3

1002   Benaven, Jean Michel. Le Caissier Italien, ou l'art de connoitre toutes les Monnaies actuelles d'Italie ; ainsi que celles de tous les etats et Princes de l'Europe. Quite two-thirds of the work are devoted to Italian coinages, Venice, Naples, Papal, &c. Vol. I consists of 347 pp., text and tables ; vol. II, of 173 plates and index. Folio, boards. Lyons, 1789.   2

1003   Birchall, S. Provincial Copper Coins and Tokens issued between the years 1786 and 1796. 141 pp. Small 8vo, half morocco. Leeds, 1796. Rare.   1

1004   Bizot, M. Histoire Metallique de la Republique de Hollande. Finely executed illustrations throughout the text, and embellished with additional appropriate ornamental designs. 317 pp., with index. Folio, full vellum. Paris, 1687.   1

1005 Bizot, M. Histoire Metallique de la Republique de Hollande. 327 pp. 104 plates. Small 8vo, full vellum. Amsterdam, 1688.　1

1006 — Histoire Metallique de la Republique de Hollande. With supplement. About 500 pp. Many plates and engravings. Incomplete. Calf and boards. Amsterdam, 1688–90.　2

1007 Blades, Wm. A List of Medals, Jetons, Tokens, etc., in connection with Printers and the Art of Printing. xv and 128 pp. 87 plates, each representing one piece. Small 8vo, cloth. London, 1869. Rare.　1

1008 Bolzenthal, Heinrich. Skizzen zur Kunstgeschichte der Modernen Medaillen — arbeit. (1429–1840). 328 pp. 30 plates. 8vo, boards. Berlin, 1844.　1

1009 Boutkowski, A. Dictionnaire Numismatique des Médailles Romaines Impériales and Grecques Coloniales. 9 parts, containing double-column pages, numbered to 1791. Royal 8vo, paper. Leipsic, 1877 to 1884.　9

1010 Boyne, Wm. The Silver Tokens of Great Britain and Ireland, the Dependencies and Colonies. 68 pp. Extra copy, printing on one side of leaf only. 7 plates. 4to, cloth. London, 1866.　1

1011 — Tokens issued in the Seventeenth Century in England, Wales and Ireland by Corporations, Merchants, Tradesmen, etc. 631 pp. 42 plates. Large 8vo, cloth. London, 1858.　1

1012 Burn, J. H. A Descriptive Catalogue of the London Traders, Tavern and Coffee House Tokens current in the 17th Century. 287 pp. Engravings. 8vo, cloth. London, 1855.　1

1013 Bushnell, Chas. I. An Arrangement of Tradesmen's Cards, Political Tokens, Election Medals, Medalets, etc., current in the U. S. of America for the last sixty years. 118 pp. 4 plates. 8vo, half morocco. New York, 1858. Rare.　1

1014 Canadian Antiquarian and Numismatic Journal. Vols. I to VIII. 780 pp. Numerous illustrations of Medals, views and portraits. 8vo, half morocco. Montreal, 1872–1880.　4

1015 Cappe, Heinrich Philipp. Die Münzen der deutschen Kaiser und Könige des Mittelalters. 3 parts. xvi and 554 pp. 39 plates. 8vo, extra half morocco. Dresden, 1848–57.　1

1016 Cardonnel, Adam de. Numismata Scotiæ, or a series of the Scottish Coinage from the Reign of William the Lion, to the Union. 180 pp., with appendix. 20 plates. Large 4to, full calf. A fine copy. Edinburgh, 1786.   1

1017 Cardwell, E. Coinage of the Greeks and Romans. 8vo, cloth. 238 pp. Oxford, 1833.   1

1018 Carlisle, Nicholas. A Memoir of the Life and Works of William Wyon, Chief Engraver of the Royal Mint; with several autograph letters of the author, and portrait and autograph letter of Mr. Wyon. 293 pp. 8vo, half morocco. An interesting compilation. London, 1837.   1

1019 Carter, Thomas. Medals of the British Army, and how they were won. 192 pp. Many illustrations of medals, with their ribbons in colors. Large 8vo, extra, cloth. London, 1861.   1

1020 Catalogue of American Store Cards, etc., issued under the auspices of the Numismatic Society of Philadelphia. Interleaved, margins for annotations. 4to. Half morocco, extra.   1

1021 — Greek Coins in the British Museum. Italy. Reginald S. Poole. 8vo, cloth (as are the rest of the series following). viii and 432 pp. Numerous engravings throughout the text. London, 1873.   1

1022 — Macedonia, etc. lxiii and 200 pp. Map and numerous engravings throughout the text. London, 1879.   1

1023 — The Ptolemies, Kings of Egypt. ciii and 136 pp. 31 plates. London, 1883.   1

1024 — Thessaly to Ætolia. lviii and 234 pp. 32 plates. London, 1883.   1

1025 — Central Greece. lxviii and 158 pp. 24 plates. London, 1884.   1

1026 — Greek Coins of Crete and the Ægean Islands. l and 152 pp. 29 plates. London, 1886.   1

1027 — Indian Coins in the British Museum. The Coins of the Sultans of Delhi. By Stanley Lane Poole. xliv and 198 pp. 9 plates. 8vo, cloth. London, 1885.   1

1028 — Coins of the Mohammedan States of India. By Stanley Lane Poole. lxx and 239 pp. 8vo, cloth. London, 1885.   1

1029 Catalogue of Coins of the Greek and Scythic Kings of
Bactria and India. By Percy Gardner. 193 pp. 31 plates.
8vo, cloth. London, 1886.   1

1030 — Oriental Coins in the British Museum. By Stanley Lane
Poole. Vol. I. 8vo, in cloth (as are the rest of the series
following, several of which are out of print, and the work
is rare). The Coins of the Eastern Khaleefehs. xx and
263 pp. 8 autotype plates. London, 1875.   1

1031 — Vol. II. Coins of the Mohammedan Dynasties. 279 pp.
8 plates. London, 1876.   1

1032 — Vol. III. Coins of the Turkuman Houses of Seljook,
Urtuk, Zengee, etc. xxvii and 305 pp. 12 plates. London, 1887.   1

1033 — Vol. IV. The Coinage of Egypt, under the Fatima Khaleefehs, the Ayyoobees, and Memlook Sultans. xxx and
279 pp. 8 plates. London, 1879.   1

1034 — Vol. V. Coins of the Moors of Africa and Spain, and the
Kings and Imams of the Yemen. xlvii and 175 pp. 7
plates. London, 1880.   1

1035 — Vol. VI. Coins of the Mongols. lxxv and 300 pp. 9
plates. London, 1881.   1

1036 — Vol. VII. Coinage of Bukhara (Transoxiana). From
the time of Timur to the present day. xlviii and 131 pp.
5 plates. London, 1882.   1

1037 — Vol. VIII. Coins of the Turks. xliii and 431 pp. 12
plates. London, 1883.   1

1038 — Additions to the Oriental Collection, Part I, supplementary to vols. I–IV of the preceding. xxiii and 405 pp. 20
plates. London, 1889.   1

1039 — Part II. Supplementary to vols. V to VIII of the preceding. xv and 206 and cclxxi pp. 33 plates. London,
1890.   1

1040 Chinese Coins. Coins of the Ta-tsíng or present dynasty of
China. Extract from the Journal of the Shanghai Lit.
and Scientific Society, pp. 43 to 202. Plates and numerous
illustrations in the text. 8vo, half morocco. Shanghai,
1858.   1

1041 Clarke, Wm. The Connexion of the Roman, Saxon and
English Coins. 552 pp., 4to, cloth. London, 1767.   1

1042   Coins of the Ancients in the British Museum.   By Barclay
       V. Head. 8vo, cloth. i to v and 128 pp. and 70 autotype
       plates. London, 1881. Volume complete and in good
       order, except that binding is loose.   .   1

1043   Coin Collectors' Journal. Vols. I to VIII. 1875 to 1883.
       Bound in 4 vols., royal 8vo, half morocco. Fine copy.
       Scott & Co. Many valuable articles, copiously illustrated.   4

1044   Conder, James. An Arrangement of Provincial Coins, To-
       kens and Medalets issued in Great Britain, Ireland and
       the Colonies, within the last twenty years. 330 pp. 3
       plates. Small 8vo, half morocco. A clean copy of a rare,
       useful and standard work. Ipswich, 1798.   1

1045   Crosby, S. S. Early Coins of America, comprising the Wash-
       ington Pieces, Anglo-American Tokens, First Patterns of
       the U. S. Mint. A very choice copy. 10 plates and the
       extra Woodburytype plate. Covers of the separate parts
       bound at the end. Extra half calf. 381 pp. Boston, 1873.   1

1046   Dickeson, M. W. The American Numismatic Manual. 270
       pp. 20 illuminated plates of fac-similes; portrait of author.
       4to, cloth. Philadelphia, 1860.   1

1047   Durand, Anthony. Médailles et Jetons des Numismates.
       246 pp. 20 plates. Large 4to, half morocco. A work of
       great interest. Geneva, 1865.   1

1048   Eckfeldt & DuBois. New varieties of Gold and Silver Coins,
       Counterfeit Coins, &c. 12mo, half morocco. 61 pp. En-
       graving of Phila. Mint. Plate of gilt California and Mor-
       mon Coins. Philadelphia, 1850.   1

1049   — New Varieties of Gold and Silver Coins. 91 pp. 5 plates.
       8vo, half morocco. New York, 1852.   1

1050   Edwards, Edward. A brief descriptive catalogue of the med-
       als struck in France and its dependencies between the
       years 1789 and 1830, contained in the cabinet of the Brit-
       ish Museum. 129 pp. 8vo, half morocco. London, 1837.   1

1051   — The Napoleon Medals. A complete series of the medals
       struck in France, Italy, Great Britain and Germany, from
       the commencement of the Empire in 1804 to the Restora-
       tion in 1815. Beautifully illustrated by the process of
       Achilles Collas, with Historical and Biographical Notices.
       168 pp. 40 plates. Folio, half sheep. London, 1837.   1

1052 Evelyn, J. A Discourse of Medals, Antient and Modern. 342 pp. and index. 99 illustrations. Small folio, extra full calf. Very choice and desirable. No finer copy can exist. London, 1697.   1

1054 Fach, E. Chur Bayrische Münzen. 967 pp. and index. 25 plates. 12mo, full calf. Leipsic, 1755.   1

1055 Felt, Jos. B. An Historical Account of Massachusetts Currency from 1628 to 1838, including the paper issues and an extended view of the Pine-tree money. The later observations have many interesting notes touching upon the Hard Times period. 248 pp. 8vo, cloth. Boston, 1839.   1

1056 — An Historical Account of Massachusetts Currency. 259 pp. 2 cuts. Half morocco. Boston : Printed by Perkins & Marvin, 1839.   1

1057 Fleurimont, G. R. Médailles du Regne de Louis XV. 54 medals described, with handsome engraving of each enclosed in an ornate frame. Large 4to, boards.   1

1058 Folkes, Martin. A Table of English Silver Coins, from the Norman Conquest to the present time. 173 pp. 61 finely engraved plates (used by Mr. Ruding in his noted work). Royal 4to, half morocco, boards. London, 1745.   1

1059 Frossard, Ed. Monograph of U. S. Cents and Half Cents, issued between the years 1793 and 1857. 58 pp. 9 plates. 4to, half calf, extra. Irvington, 1879.   1

1060 Gibson, J. H. British Military and Naval Medals and Decorations. 141 pp. Large 8vo, cloth. London, 1880.   1

1061 Grueber, Herbert A. A Guide to the English Medals exhibited in the King's Library. 8vo, boards. i to xxi and 172 pp. and 7 autotype plates. London, 1881.   1

1062 Hawkins, Edward. The Silver Coins of England. 308 pp. 47 plates. Large 8vo, cloth. Binding loose. London. 1841. 1

1063 Heath, L. Infallible Government Counterfeit Detector, with illustrations from the original plates. 39 pp. 4to, full cloth. Boston and Washington, 1867.   1

1064 Henfrey, H. W. A Guide to the Study and Arrangement of English Coins. 180 pp. Illus. 8vo, cloth. London, 1870.   1

1065 — Numismata Cromwelliana, or the Medallic History of Oliver Cromwell. 230 pp. 8 fine autotype plates. 4to, half calf. A perfect copy of a fine work. London, 1877.   1

1066 Hennin, M.   Histoire Numismatique de la Revolution Fran-
çaise.   705 pp.   95 plates.   4to, half morocco, cloth.
Paris, 1826.   2

1067 Heraeus, Carl Gustav.   Thesaurus Numismatum Modern-
orum Hujus Seculi.   1097 pp., besides index.   Text in
Latin and German.   Copiously illustrated.   Small folio,
calf.   Nuremburg, 1716.   1

1068 Hickcox, John H.   An Historical Account of American Coinage.   153 pp.   5 plates.   Large 8vo, half morocco.   Al-
bany, 1858.   1

1069 — A History of the Bills of Credit or Paper Money issued
by New York from 1709 to 1789, with a description of the
bills and catalogue of the various issues.   Royal 8vo, half
calf, extra.   Albany, 1866.   1

1070 Hirsch, Alexander.   Die Medaillen auf den Entsatz Wiens,
1683.   35 pp.   8 plates.   4to, half morocco.   Troppau, 1883.   1

1071 Humphreys, H. N.   The Coin Collectors' Manual, or Guide
to the Numismatic Student in the Formation of a Cabinet
of Coins.   726 pp.   10 plates.   With valuable tables of explanations of Greek and Roman inscriptions, &c.   London,
1853.   2

1072 — The Coins of England.   120 pp.   23 illuminated plates.
Fancy gilt boards ; back slightly defective ; a few leaves
loose.   London, 1846.   1

1073 — The Gold, Silver and Copper Coins of England.   136 pp.
24 plates in colors.   Small 8vo, half mor.   London, 1849.   1

1074 Jennings, Rev. David.   An Introduction to the Knowledge of
Medals.   Small 8vo, half calf.   59 pp.   Birm., 1775.   1

1075 Jennings, Hargrave.   One of the Thirty — (pieces of silver
for which Jesus Christ was sold).   A strange history now
for the first time told.   359 pp.   Illustrated.   Small 8vo,
cloth.   London.   1

1076 Johnson, Edwin L.   J. A. Bolen's Medals, Cards and Fac-
Similes.   14 pp.   8vo, cloth.   Springfield, Mass., 1882.   1

1077 Juncker, Christian.   Das Guldene und Silberne Ehren-Be-
dachtniss des Theuren Gottes-Lehrers D. Martini Lutheri,
&c.   562 pp.   Index, numerous illustrations, and portrait
of Luther.   Small 8vo, half sheep, boards.   Frankfort and
Leipsic, 1706.   1

1078 King, C. W. Early Christian Numismatics. 324 pp. 1 plate. 8vo, full cloth. London, 1873.   1

1079 Kohlers, Johann David. Historischer Munz-Belustigung. 24 parts in 12 vols. Small 4to. Finely bound in full vellum. Engraved portrait of the author. Filled throughout with handsome plates and engravings in the text. Each part contains about 450 pp. A superb work, in perfect condition ; no finer copy can exist. Nuremberg, 1729–1764.   12

1080 Kreusler, M. H. G. D. Martin Luther's Undenken in Münzen. 152 pp. 44 plates. 8vo, boards. Leipsic, 1818.   1

1081 Kundmann, J. C. (Medical Doctor in Breslau). Nummi Singulares oder Sonderhare Thaler und Munzen. 152 pp. 5 plates. Small 4to, boards. Breslau, 1731.   1

1082 Laskey, J. C. Medals of Napoleon Bonaparte. Large 8vo, boards. 239 pp. London, 1818.   1

1083 Le Blanc, M. Traité Historique des Monnoyes de France. (From the commencement of the Monarchy to the present time — 1703). Numerous plates and tables. 4to, full calf. 436 pp. Paris, 1703.   1

1084 Le Fèvre, Theodore. Tableau des Monnaies d'or et d'argent. Small 8vo, half morocco. 72 pp. 30 plates, with coins in metal colors. Paris.   1

1085 Lenormant, C. Nouvelle Galérie Mythologique. Supplement to the "Tresor Numismatique." 80 plates of ancient Greek and Roman Coins, including 8 of Bactria, with text. lx and 116 pp. Folio, half sheep, boards. No date, but subsequent to 1835.   1

1086 Lenormant, Fr. Monnaies et Médailles. 317 pp. 151 engravings. 8vo, half morocco. Paris, about 1880.   1

1087 Lochner, J. H. Samlung Merkwurdiger Medallen. 1280 pp., besides extensive indices. Many beautiful engravings. Small 4to, full vellum. Nuremburg, 1737–1739.   1

1088 Lohner, Carl. Die Münzen der Republik Bern. 270 pp. 2 plates. 8vo, half morocco. Zurich, 1846.   1

1089 Madden, Fred W. The Handbook of Roman Numismatics. 172 pp. 6 plates. Small 8vo, cloth. London, 1861.   1

1090 — Coins of the Jews. 329 pp. 279 wood-cuts and a plate of alphabets. Large 4to, cloth. London, 1881. Published at $12.   1

1091 Magnau, D. Bruttia Numismatica ; seu Bruttiæ, hodie Cal-
abriæ, Populorum Numismata Omnia. 12 pp. 51 plates.
Folio, full vellum, flexible cover. Rome, 1773.   1

1092 Maris, Edward, M. D. Varieties of the Copper Issues of
the U. S. Mint in the year 1794. 1st ed. 1869, 2d ed.
1870. 15 and 16 pp. Both rare. 12mo, paper.   2

1093 Martin-Leake, Stephen. An Historical Account of English
Money from the Conquest to the present time, including
Scotland from James I. Second edition. 428 pp. 17
plates, table and index. 8vo, calf. London, 1745.   1

1094 Meadows, W. Nummi Britannici Historia : Or an Historical
Account of English Money from the Conquest, etc. 144
pp. 8 plates and index. Full calf. London, 1626.   1

1095 Mease, James, M. D., and J. S. Fisher. A Descriptive List
of American Medals. Two early and interesting extracts,
neatly made into a volume under the direction of the late
Chas. I. Bushnell, whose autograph appears on a fly-leaf.
33 pp. 8vo, half morocco. Philadelphia, 1832.   1

1096 Mechel, Chretien de. Explication Historique et Critique des
Médailles de l'œuvre du Chevalier J. C. Hedlinger, pré-
cédée de l'éloge Historique de ce célèbre artiste. xxviii
and 64 pp. 40 artistic plates. Royal 4to, calf. Basle,
1778.   1

1097 Medallic History of Napoleon, from 1796 to 1815. 41 pp.
74 finely executed plates. Large 4to, half sheep, boards,
gilt top. London, 1819.   1

1098 Mélange de Médailles. 218 plates of Ancient Greek and
Roman Coins, without text. Small folio, boards.   1

1099 Mionnet, T. E. De la Rareté et du Prix des Médailles Romaines. 3d edition. 2 vols. 938 pp. Numerous plates.
8vo, boards. Paris, 1847.   1

1100 Noble, Mark. Mint and Coins of the Episcopal–Palatines
of Durham. 91 pp. 21 plates inserted in the text. 4to,
boards. Birmingham, 1780.   1

1101 Numismatic Chronicle. 1837 to 1847. Bound in 6 vols.
Numerous plates. 8vo, half morocco. London.   6

1102 Numismata Historica Anni MDCCX. Latin and German
text in parallel columns. 78 pp. Many illustrations. Small
folio, boards. Nuremberg.   1

1103 Numismatica Veneta o Serie di Monete e Medaglie dei Dogi
      di Venezia. About 170 pp. Engravings of each piece,
      several fine plates. Small folio, half morocco, extra. Ven-
      ice, 1859.   1

1104 Pembroke, Collection of the Earl of. Ancient and Modern.
      In 3 parts and 2 volumes. 305 plates, without text. 4to,
      full calf, cover of one missing. 1747.   2

1105 Pinkerton, John. An Essay on Medals. 1st ed. 326 pp.
      Small 8vo, calf. London, 1784. 3d ed. 2 vols. 824 pp.
      5 plates and Index. London, 1808.   3

1105a — The Medallic History of England to the Revolution.
      112 pp. 40 plates. Folio, calf. London, 1790.   1

1106 Prime, W. C. Coins, Medals and Seals, Ancient and Mod-
      ern. 292 pp. 114 plates. Small 4to, cloth. New York,
      1864.   1

1107 Read, Samuel. An Essay on the Coins of Cunobelin. 136
      pp. 2 plates. 4to, full calf. Slightly defective. London,
      1766.   1

1108 Riddell, J. L. A Monograph of the Silver Dollar, Good and
      Bad, illustrated with fac-similes of 425 varieties of dollars
      and 87 varieties of half-dollars, interspersed through the
      text. 8vo, half sheep. New Orleans, 1845.   1

1109 Ruding, Rev. Rogers. Annals of the Coinage of Great Bri-
      tain and its Dependencies. Third, last and best edition.
      3 vols. Vols. I and II, 942 pp. of text, with map ; Vol.
      III, 42 plates, and as many supplementary. 4to, half mo-
      rocco, extra, marble edges. Rare and valuable. London,
      1840.   3

1110 Sandham, Alfred. Coins, Tokens and Medals of the Do-
      minion of Canada, with supplement. 175 pp. 8 plates.
      8vo, half morocco. Montreal, 1869.   1

1111 — Medals commemorative of the visit of H. R. H. the
      Prince of Wales to Montreal in 1860. Contains 13 mount-
      ed photographic plates by W. Notman, including a military
      portrait of the Prince. 56 pp. 8vo, half morocco. Mont-
      real, 1871.   1

1112 Satterlee, A. H. An Arrangement of Medals and Tokens,
      struck in honor of the Presidents of the United States.
      84 pp. 8vo, half morocco. New York, 1862.   1

1113   Sealy, H. N.   A Treatise on Coins, Currency and Banking.
       Once the property of Henry Ward Beecher, whose auto-
       graph heads the title-page.   633 pp.   8vo, cloth.   London,
       1858.   1

1114   Simon, James.   An Essay towards an Historical Account of
       Irish Coins, with supplement.   This rare edition contains
       auction catalogue of the author's collection.   204 pp.   12
       plates.   4to, full calf.   Dublin, 1749.   1

1115   Smith, Aquila, M. D.   Tradesmen's Tokens current in Ire-
       land between the years 1637 and 1679.   31 pp., with addi-
       tional blank leaves.   8vo, half morocco.   Dublin, 1849.   1

1116   Smith, Wm. Henry.   Descriptive Catalogue of a Cabinet of
       Roman Imperial Large Brass Medals.   xxii and 352 pp.
       Royal 4to, cloth.   Bedford, 1834.   1

1117   Snelling, T.   A View of the Silver Coins and Coinage of
       England from the Norman Conquest to the present time.
       91 pp.   24 plates, with a special additional plate inserted.
       Large 4to, half calf.   Front cover broken.   London, 1762.   1

1118   — Thirty-three plates of English Medals.   A rare book.
       Small folio, calf.   London, 1776.   1

1119   Snowden, J. R.   A Description of Ancient and Modern Coins
       in the cabinet collection of the Mint of the United States.
       407 pp.   27 plates of coins in relief, in color of metal.
       8vo, cloth.   Philadelphia, 1860.   1

1120   Stukeley, Rev. Dr.   Twenty-three plates of the Coins of the
       Ancient British Kings.   4to, half sheep, boards.   London.   1

1121   Souvenirs Numismatiques de la Revolution, 1848.   111 pp.
       60 plates.   4to, extra half calf.   1

1122   Till, Wm.   An Essay on the Roman Denarius and English
       Silver Penny, etc.   226 pp.   Plate.   Small 8vo, cloth.
       London, 1838.   1

1123   Tiregale, P. Rigaud de.   Médailles sur les principaux événe-
       mens de l'Empire de Russie depuis le Règne de Pierre le
       Grand jusqu'à celui de Catherine II avec des Explications
       Historiques.   116 pp.   Engraving of each medal, with a
       finely executed portrait of Catherine II facing the title-
       page.   Folio, paper.   Potsdam, 1772.   1

    Works on Russian Medals are very uncommon. This, for its period, is perhaps the
best.

1124 Walsh, Rev. R. An Essay on Ancient Coins, Medals and Gems, as Illustrating the Progress of Christianity in the Early Ages. 140 pp. 38 plates and other engravings. 12mo, half morocco. London, 1828. 1

1125 Withy and Ryall. Twelve plates of English Silver Coins from the Conquest to Henry VIII. Eight additional plates bound in. 4to, half morocco, boards. London, 1756. 1

1126 Woodward, Ashbel. Wampum. A paper read before the Numismatic and Antiquarian Society of Philadelphia. Large 8vo, cloth. 61 pp. Albany, 1878. 1

1127 Van Alkemade, Kornelis. De Goude en Zilvere Gangbaare Penningen der Graaven en Graavinnen van Holland. 192 pp. with index and table. 45 plates. Small folio, full vellum. Delft, 1700. 1

1128 Van der Chijs, P. O. Nederlandsche Munten, Tot. 1576. Braband en Limburg; Gelderland; Heeren en Steden; Overyssel; Friesland, Groningen en Drenthe; Holland en Zeeland; Utrecht; Frankische en Duitsche Nederlandsche Vorsten — text in Dutch in 9 volumes, containing up- wards of 4,000 pp. and 262 finely engraved plates. Large 4to, half calf, extra gilt top. A beautiful and valuable work, and an ornament for any library. Haarlem, 1851 to 1866. 9

1129 Van Loon, Gerard. Beschryving der Nederlandsche Histori Penningen. 4 vols., containing 2,389 pp., with innumerable finely engraved illustrations throughout the text — single and in groups — index and table of legends. A fine copy of a valuable work, in full vellum, folio. Graavenhaage, 1723-31. 4

1130 — Supplement. Vol. V, 1731-66. Printed in Amsterdam, 1821-48. 456 pp. 36 plates. Vol. VI, 1767-1806. Amsterdam, 1861. 536 and liv pp. Plates, 37-88. Half morocco, folio. Rare and valuable. 2

1131 Vergara, C. A. Monete del Regno di Napoli da Roggierio Primo Re, sino all'Augustissimo Regnante, Carlo VI Im- peradore, e III, Re Cattolico. 140 pp., with numerous illustrations throughout the text. Folio, boards. Rome, 1716. 1

1132 Verkade, P. Nederlandsche Munten. 1576–1833. A fine
      work, handsomely compiled, uniformly bound, and an ap-
      propriate sequel to the work of Van der Chijs. 214 pp.
      228 plates. Large 4to, half calf, extra, gilt top. Schiedam,
      1848.   1

1133 Vissering, W. On Chinese Currency. Coin and Paper
      Money. 219 pp. A few illustrations with fac simile of a
      bank note. 8vo, cloth. Leiden, 1877.   1

1134 **Miscellaneous.** Browning, Decimal system ; Bodemann &
      Kerl, Essay ; Cappe, Mittelalter Munzen (Munster, Osna-
      bruck, etc.) The Coin Book (Numismatic Dictionary and
      23 plates).   4

1135 Imlay & Bicknell. Coins of the world (plates) ; Kundmann,
      Nummi Singulares (3 plates); Le Roux, Numismatic Atlas ;
      Smith, A. M., U. S. Mint ; Stainsfield, Australian Trades-
      men's Tokens ; Ogden, Tables of Foreign Moneys re-
      duced into dollars and cents ; Wells, D. A., Robinson
      Crusoe's Money (illustrated by Nast).   7

1136 **In Paper.** Appleton, Medals of Washington ; 24 pp., 1873 ;
      Bagehot, Plan for Assimilating English and American
      Money, 70 pp., 1869 ; Betts, Counterfeit Halfpence cur-
      rent in American Colonies, 17 pp. 1886 ; Bushnell, Early
      New York Tokens, 15 pp., 1859 ; Delmar, A., Monograph
      of the History of Money in China. 34 pp. 2 plates.
      1881.   5

1137 Breton, Coins and Tokens of Canada, 240 pp. 1894 ; Kings-
      ford, Wm., A Canadian Political Coin (Vexator Canaden-
      sis) 24 pp., rare ; McLachlan, Canadian Numismatic Bibli-
      ography, 16 pp., 1886 ; also Coins, Medals and Tokens of
      the Dominion of Canada, 127 pp. 1886.   4

1138 Hart, Paper Money in the Colonies anterior to the Revolu-
      tion, 20 pp., 1851 ; Lawrence, Medals of Giovanni Cavino,
      31 pp., 1883 ; Phillips, Paper Money issued by Pennsyl-
      vania, 40 pp., 1862 ; also Notes upon Coins in Penn.
      Museum, 15 pp., 1879.   4

1139 Satterlee, Presidential Medals and Tokens, 84 pp., 1862 ;
      Wharton, Small Money and Nickel Alloy Coinage, 50 pp.,
      37 illustrations, 1877 ; Zabriskie, Political and Memorial
      Medals of Lincoln, 32 pp., 1873.   3

1140 **Pamphlets.** Letter from the Secretary of State, enclosing Report of the Director of the Mint, 1796; another, 1797; also a plan for a General Print-Mint at Washington for the emission of Paper Money, Charleston, 1837; and others, various, relating to the U. S. Mints, Coinage Laws, etc., down to 1870. Some are rare. 13

1141 — Continental Paper Money; Hog Money of the Somers Islands; Satterlee on Presidentials; Warner, Communion Tokens; Low on Morelos, etc., including a short address to Amer. Coin Collectors, which will readily be recognized as from the pen of our interesting and very candid friend in Birmingham (well known to American dealers). 14

1142 Periodicals. Decorah, Iowa; Curiosity Hunter, Rockford, Ill.; American Antiquarian; Mason's Coin and Stamp Magazine; Steigerwalt's Coin Journal; Coin Collector's Journal, etc., from 8vo to 4to. Paper. 135

1143 Dealers' Catalogues; Continental and Colonial Notes; Confederate Notes, including Chase's Catalogue of the Rebellion Tokens of 1861, and Dalton's Catalogue of British War Medals, 1874, etc. 17

AMERICAN AUCTION CATALOGUES.

Uniformly bound in half morocco, lettered on back, with name and date. Some priced, marked with *; others priced and named, marked with † (including a few of the neatest specimens of penmanship I have ever met with).

1144 1855 Flandin,† Cline.* Rare. 2
1145 1858 Cogan, Norton, May* and Oct.† 3
1146 1859 Bangs, Merwin & Co., June† and Dec.*; Bogert,† Bramhall,† Foskett,† Levick,† Whitmore.† 7
1147 1860 Bangs, Merwin & Co.,† Bramhall,† Cogan,† May,† June* and Oct.†; Curtis, Nov. and Dec.†; Draper, Morse & Co.* 8
1148 Gallagher,† Groh,† Hewett,† Hill, April† and Sept.†; Morse,† Leonard,* Prime and Haines,† Wiggin.* 9
1149 1861 B., M. & Co.,† King, Lamb & Co.,* Leonard,* Piazzi,† Robinson, Jan. and May; † Wildey. 8
1150 1862 B., M. & Co., Mch., Apl., May,† Aug.,* Sept.; Cook,* Davis.* 7

1151 Fleury,† Lilliendahl,† Robinson, Mch.† and May *; Satter-
      lee,* Woodward,† Young.   7

1152 1863 B., M. & Co., Feb.,† May, June, Dec.; Bridgens,* Co-
      gan,* Haines.*   7

1153 Harrison,† Jackson,† Jewell,* Leavitt, Leeds & Co., Sept.,
      Nov., Dec.; Leonard & Co.   8

1154 Lilliendahl,† Muhlenberg,† Seavey,† Smith,* Wall & Co.,
      Woodward, May † and Dec.†   7

1155 1864 Beckford, July 13 and 27,* Sept., Dec.; Blake, Cogan,
      Jan.† and June.†   7

1156 Cooley,† Hubbard, Leeds & Miner, Leonard & Co., Jan.,*
      May,* Nov.†; Riley.*   7

1157 McCoy, John F., by W. Elliot Woodward, May 17 to 21, 3122
      lots. A choice copy, artistically priced and named, with
      cat. of C. Wyllys Betts' Collection, sold May 4, bound in.
      Rare.   1

1158 McGilvray, April and Oct.; Prince, Seavey, Woodward,
      March and Oct.†   6

1159 1865 B., M. & Co., Cogan, Conant & S., Edwards, Haines,
      Hatch, Hageman & Co. (the last two broadsides, v. rare),
      Woodward, Thomas & Sons, McGilvray.   10

1160 1866 Birch & Son, March and May; Chambers; Hatch,
      Feb. and Oct.; Hoffman, Jenks & Paine, Leonard & Co.,
      Lightbody, Rosenthal.*   10

1161 1867 B., M. & Co., January, March and September; Birch
      & Son, Borg, Chadbourne,* Woodward, Zanoni &
      Bogert.   8

1162 Mickley, Jos. J., New York, Oct. 27. 3349 lots, priced and
      named. Among the most prominent of American Coin
      Sales.   1

1163 1868 L. S. & Co., June and Dec.; Mackenzie, Nippes, Oliver
      two, one unpriced, the other differently bound, priced
      and named), Randall.   7

1164 Dealers' Catalogues. 1858 Curtis, N. Y.; Whipple &
      Son, Salem, Mass.; 1859, Curtis; Sage, N. Y., February
      and June; 1860, Dayton, N. Y.; 1861, De Haven,
      Philadelphia; Robinson, Hartford, June, July; 1862, Curtis,
      N. Y.   10

PRICED CATALOGUES UNBOUND.

1165 1858, '59, (3), '60 (16). 20

1166 1861 (4), '62 (10) including Finotti; '63 (including Mary Anne Bacon, Broadside), Haines, Lilliendahl, etc. (16). 30

1167 1864 Including the McCoy and the Thos. Riley. 12

The Riley Catalogue informs us that this gentlemen (regarding whom see note following Lot 226), was also a coin collector, and that this sale contained the " Celebrated, valuable and rare collection of Coins, Medals, Autographs, Continental Paper Money, Newspapers, Engravings, Paintings, relics of Washington, etc., of the late Mr. Thomas Riley of the Fifth Ward Museum Hotel, New York."

1168 1865 Including Chilton, Edwards and Woodward's 6th and 7th semi-annuals. 7

1169 1866 (4), '67 (3), '68 (2), '69, including the Mackenzie, with plates, artistically priced and named (4). 13

1170 1870 (2), '71, including the Clay, with plates ; Upton Chicago sale, Gov. Packer (8), '72 (2), '73 (5), '74 (7), including Balmanno, Sanford, Parker, etc. 24

1171 1875 Including Col. Cohen, Stenz, Jewett, etc. 11

1172 1876 (15), '77 (14), including Da Silva, Adams, Farrier, Ferguson Haines, etc. 29

1173 1878 Including Snow and Redlich (with plates), Clemens, Holland, Root, etc. 16

1174 1879 Including Anthon, Michael Moore, Pratt, Robinson, etc. 32

1175 1880 Including Bispham, Ferguson Haines, Jenks, Anthon ; also Pittsburgh, Baltimore and Lancaster sales, and Haseltine's Type Table (42), '82 (4), '83 (2), '88 (2), including Ely's U. S. Gold Coins, G. E. Hart. Several in heavy paper. 50

1176 1882 Woodward, June 6 and 7, July 11 and 12, Oct. 16 to 18, Dec. 11 and 12, 28 and 29. All with plates and extra paper copies. A select lot. 5

1177 Unbound and Unpriced. Plate catalogues, mostly in heavy paper, 1869 to 1889. Including Cohen, Mackenzie, Levick (store cards, May, '84), Chubbuck, Seavey, Balmanno and Allen. A clean and choice lot. 30

1178 Another lot : 1882 (4), '83 (2). 6

1179 Large 4to, 1860, Cogan, (printed prices), '70, Birch, Fewsmith.
      '82, Bushnell (printed prices, 12 plates). '84, Warner, print-
      ed prices, 12 plates. '89, Davis, priced, 4 plates, in fine
      order, fine lot and very desirable.   6

1180 Parmelee, L. G. Catalogue of the valuable and well-known
      collection. Bound copy, unpriced. 12 plates, in colors,
      and photograph of Mr. Parmelee. June, 1890.   1

1181 Catalogues, unpriced, 1864 to '93, mostly after '90.   30

1182 Foreign Catalogues (auction), Dutch, German and Italian,
      including the Morbio Collection, valuable for Italian
      money, and Mr. Montague's Collection of Patterns and
      Proofs of the Coinages of the British Possessions and
      Colonies, 1892 (the latter a rare assemblage).   16

1183 Dealers' Lists and Catalogues, mostly German.   50

227

11

21

158

34

154

198

49

97

121

132

133

163

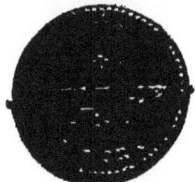
77

180

167

175

28

177

179

225

79

202

205

222

223

229 238 245 233

273 334 571 581

521 567 522

392 393 394 520

287 275 387

PLATE 2.

302a

125

878

239a   81

PLATE 3.